THE AFRICAN NETTLE

THE

AFRICAN

NETTLE

*Dilemmas of an
Emerging Continent*

EDITED BY Frank S. Meyer

Essay Index Reprint Series

BOOKS FOR LIBRARIES PRESS
FREEPORT, NEW YORK

INTERNATIONAL STANDARD BOOK NUMBER:

0-8369-1764-2

LIBRARY OF CONGRESS CATALOG CARD NUMBER:

78-121488

PRINTED IN THE UNITED STATES OF AMERICA

. . . Out of this nettle, danger, we pluck this flower, safety.
Henry iv, Part i

Contents

INTRODUCTORY

1   The Prickly Dilemmas

—————

Frank S. Meyer

FRANK S. MEYER, *born in Newark, New Jersey, in 1909, was educated at Princeton University and Balliol College, Oxford, where he took his B.A. and M.A. He pursued additional studies at the London School of Economics and the University of Chicago.*

A senior editor of National Review, *he has written* The Moulding of Communists *(1961) and* In Defense of Freedom *(1962); he edited the volume,* What Is Conservatism? *(1964). His forthcoming book will be entitled* The Dynamics of American History. *He also lectures widely.*

The very rapid changes that have taken place in Africa in the last decade have catapulted that continent, for so long remote from current world affairs, into the most prominent spot on earth, to judge from the volume of discussion concerning it. This torrent of words flows for the most part in one mighty stream of denunciation of colonialism, of the "historic wrongs" done to the black peoples of the earth. Emotional fervor carries all before it, with the result that very little dispassionate analysis exists, much less any reasoned or objective approach to what in fact the actual

11

problems of that continent are or what solutions are possible.

The authors of these essays, although they range all along the political spectrum, lower the temperature of this fevered discourse. They all have intimate knowledge of Africa, either as natives, or as longtime residents of African countries, or as close students and observers of African affairs. Because they are all deeply concerned for the well-being of Africa, they use reason, not emotion, to assess the situation; they consider possible solutions under concrete circumstances, instead of concocting unrealistic and soul-satisfying abstractions to fit Utopian preconceptions.

Reasoned dialogue needs to replace frenzied monologue on Africa. This volume is an attempt to begin that dialogue. There is, of course, no "Africa" in a political sense, only an enormous and enormously complex continent made up of areas in widely different stages of economic, political, and social development. Yet we speak of "Africa," meaning sub-Saharan Africa, and in his brilliant opening essay, Gilbert Comte analyzes the factors that do prevail throughout and give meaning to that usage. His dissection of the inner logic of colonialism, as of the inevitable frustrations of decolonization and the faulty responses to those frustrations, lays bare the psychological realities which are critical for understanding current development.

Further illumination of the background is provided by Professor P. T. Bauer, a world authority on the economics of underdeveloped countries. He presents a convincing refutation of the widely accepted thesis (and the one favored by the United Nations) of "the vicious circle of poverty and stagnation," which, as he remarks, "is in flagrant contradiction to logic and obvious empirical evidence." Professor Bauer also explodes a number of other myths: that Africans do not respond to economic incentives; that

Africans do not look ahead; that Africans are not entrepreneurs; that poverty precludes economic advance; that rapid progress is impossible without industrialization. While stressing the variety and complexity in such a huge and heterogeneous area as Africa, he finds "its economies do exhibit certain features in common which justify limited generalizations for certain purposes." The "limited generalizations" which he offers put the African economic picture into perspective. The problems of Africa are *not* those of stagnation, but of rapid growth and change.

Mrs. Elspeth Huxley completes the overall view with a careful analysis of the actual process of disengagement of the European powers from Africa. Whatever the policies of the respective powers had been—the French and Portuguese assimilationist approach, the Belgian road of economic progress before political development, or the British path of indirect rule and training for self-government—all have foundered on the psychological rocks already noted by M. Comte. Change has become revolutionary, not evolutionary. All "gradualism" has been swept away, along with the qualified franchise, "multiracialism," and the legitimate claims of immigrant communities, Indian as well as European. Mrs. Huxley makes a trenchant survey of the immediate consequences and refrains from predicting the long-range effects.

The passionate intensity of what she calls the "two communities," indigenous and immigrant, is reflected in the contributions of Mr. Busia of Ghana and Sir Roy Welensky of Southern Rhodesia. Despite Mr. Busia's misgivings about one-party regimes, he shares the deep sentiments that have propelled Africa on a revolutionary course, while Sir Roy argues with sincerity and eloquence for the evolutionary course now being abandoned. The view of an outside but acute observer is contributed by Professor

Thomas Molnar who has just traveled extensively in Africa and intensively investigated its prevailing realities.

The intensities reach incandescent heat, of course, in South Africa, and here especially all dispassionate analysis has been engulfed in a sea of emotionalism. The most obvious factors, which set South Africa off as a unique case, are usually not even mentioned. (1) The Afrikaners do not represent a European power; they are not colonialists in the current sense, having settled in South Africa at the time North America was being colonized and at the time the Bantus were only beginning to come into the area from the North. (2) South Africa is a developed, not an underdeveloped country.

Starting from this incontrovertible factual basis, both Mr. Giniewski and Professor Hutt address themselves to the problem of establishing racial justice in South Africa. Both condemn present policies and offer totally fresh and imaginative approaches in the extremely complex situation. Their sometimes startling statements shake the mind out of accustomed grooves and force the subject of South Africa into new and sharper focus.

If there is one theme emerging from these essays, it is the tragedy of impatience—understandable, perhaps, but still a tragedy. There is agreement that the new nationalist leaders are embarked on a course ruinous to the continued development and well-being of Africa. African "nations" do not in reality exist; there are as yet only attempts to create them out of former administrative areas superimposed on the remnants of a tribal structure. What does exist is "African nationalism" which has meant racial nationalism and Pan-African aggressive intentions. Neither of these is conducive to the technological progress so ardently proclaimed by the nationalist leaders as their goal. Cooperation of black and white in some form is indispensable if the newly created states are not to slip sharply backward. There does not exist at present anything like a sufficient number of qualified black Africans to train the personnel for a technological society, or even to administer *any* form of government other than the traditional tribal form; and "tribalism," as Mrs. Huxley points out, has now become a dirty word.

Is there, then, any solution for the dilemmas of Africa? The automatic answer is: the United Nations. Mr. Lessing and Mr. Valahu weigh this question. Mr. Lessing in measured terms renders a carefully qualified verdict for a positive and limited role for the United Nations; Mr. Valahu enters a harsh dissent, using the United Nations' role in the Congo as a test case. Every contributor to the volume touches upon the role of the United Nations in Africa and every one has reservations, ranging from Mr. Busia's troubled concern over the promotion of ends inimical to freedom to the forthright conclusion of most that the United Nations has been an Iago, a goad and spur in bringing the tragedy of impatience to swift crisis.

The consensus is that the United Nations, far from being the automatic answer, is a most unsatisfactory answer. If the continent is to be saved from chaos—and from Communist capitalization on chaos—some form of concerted Western action is imperative. Mr. Lessing phrases it somewhat optimistically:

Owing to the deeply conflicting attitudes of the major Western powers, the United Nations' approach to Africa so far has been less constructive than it could have been. But it is not yet too late for a change to be made. A first essential, however, must be a determination on the part of the more responsible members of the United Nations not to be so easily browbeaten by the more exuberantly fanatical representatives of the smaller African nations who seek to use the United Nations as a sounding board to bolster their own ego. A beginning could be made if more Western leaders will admit that Africa is a more complicated continent than they had realized and that there are no easy solutions to the many problems, and that many of the African delegates do not represent the fount of all wisdom concerning Africa. And that this also applies to Western delegates, many of whom have never seen Africa or who have merely been taken on a conducted tour of the showplaces.

M. Comte puts it more bluntly: "If the disorders in Africa are to be mastered it must be by a global strategy. Nothing of importance will be accomplished so long as Washington, London, and Paris do not agree on a common policy. To place our hopes for a solution in the United Nations would be, as the Congo has so graphically demonstrated, an expensive and disappointing waste of time."

It is clear from a reading of these essays that there *are* answers to the problems of Africa and that these answers are not tied to any quixotic or nostalgic notions of restoring the former status, with its good as well as its bad points. "Neo-colonialism" is a bogeyman, not a real threat; cooperation of black and white is a dire necessity. Whether cool heads will prevail over emotion is an entirely different question. They often do not in the affairs of men. In that case, the possible solutions will not be exploited; the consequences no one can foretell, except that they will probably not be happy for Africa, for the free world, for world peace.

AN OVERVIEW

2 # The Psychological Realities
of Africa

GILBERT COMTE

GILBERT COMTE, *born in Paris in 1932, is a professional journalist. He has written widely on the problems of Africa and on Communism. His reportage and political analysis have appeared in diverse journals: the monthly* Le Spectacle du Monde; Europe-France-Outremer, *the oldest French monthly devoted to Africa; the leftist North African weekly,* Jeune Afrique; *the rightist weekly,* La Nation Française; *the daily* Le Monde. *In 1963 he received the Prix Pierre Mille for the best articles appearing on Africa during the year.*

In the course of his frequent trips to the African states of the Ivory Coast, Dahomey, Congo-Leopoldville, Congo-Brazzaville, Togo, Upper Volta, Niger, Mauritania, Senegal, Algeria, and Morocco, he has met and talked with the dominant African leaders, including Presidents Senghor, Houphouët-Boigny, and Moise Tshombe.

He is also the author of a book on Soviet history, La Révolution Russe par Ses Témoins, *published in Paris in 1963.*

For more than a century, Africa caused no trouble to Europe or America. It seemed to inhabitants of Paris, Lon-

don and New York that life went on in the tropics according to a simple and agreeable design: altruistic white men
carried the marvels of "civilization" to the black man. Following in the steps of intrepid explorers and devoted missionaries, these pioneers cleared the jungles, built hospitals
in unhealthy countries and set up schools for backward
peoples.

Between 1880 and 1945, this division of roles seemed
destined to continue for a long time to come. The colonial
powers believed in their humanitarian mission. In exchange, they expected from the natives eternal obedience
and gratitude. There seemed little doubt that this white
domination, accompanied as it was by great technical superiority, would continue. No one could imagine that
these poor subject populations, without arms or money,
with no experience in government, would one day dare to
pull free of the domination of the industrialized nations of
the West.

The Africans had, for a long time, justified these expectations by their actions. When conflict erupted in the
Cameroons in 1911, it was not between local nationalists
and foreign conquerors but between two of the conquerors, France and Germany. During that period the major
rivalries on the Dark Continent merely mirrored disputes
among various European nations and were settled thousands of miles away. The peoples of the colonies were, by
and large, indifferent to these quarrels. They took part in
them sometimes, but only in an ancillary capacity.

Resistance and uprisings had, to be sure, dotted the path
of the colonizers. Samory Touré, the grandfather of the
present president of the Republic of Guinea, Sékou Touré,
fought for seven years against the French in an area ranging from the sources of the Niger to the heights of the
Ivory Coast. Before him, the Toucouleurs of Senegal and
Ahmadou bands in the Sudan had bravely defended their

territories. At Dahomey, King Béhanzin held off European assaults until 1892. Troops sent from France waged their last great battle in 1900 on the banks of Lake Chad and killed the Moslem chief Rabah.

But it is important not to exaggerate the political significance of these long campaigns. They were fought by second-line troops. The black chiefs were motivated less by the ideal of independence than by a desire to safeguard their commercial interests in the slave trade. Even the most ferocious among them, Samory, Béhanzin and Rabah, frequently tried to treat with the whites in order to maintain their slaving interests. They were not animated by any nationalist ideals. Indeed, the peoples they captured looked upon the Europeans as liberators, and the newcomers found it easy to recruit volunteers and guides among the oppressed tribes. As soldiers, the natives proved faithful to the death to the new masters they had chosen. The history of colonialism abounds in acts of heroism by native troops in battle against other Africans. To mention only one episode, in 1907 twenty Senegalese riflemen, after the death of their French captain, decapitated through treachery, held off for fifteen days an entire army which was besieging them at Zinder.

Further, there was not a single bloody revolt in the European colonies in Africa during the Second World War. In the French territories men enlisted by the thousands to defend Metropolitan France. During the four years of the German occupation, the tricolor of France flew from Dakar to Brazzaville—long after it had disappeared in Paris. Never did the Negroes take advantage of the disaster of the mother country to try to win their independence. The belief that white domination would continue was seemingly not unfounded. What, then, in the succeeding years so changed the course of African history?

*   *   *

The basic cause of this reversal lies in the nature of colonialism itself. Its own inner logic led to the formation of modern elites, the seeds of its destruction. Prejudices, on both sides, tend to obscure the analysis of this situation. For the professional anti-colonialist, the European domination was little more than the unscrupulous exploitation of an oppressed people. For the fanatic disciple of the *status quo*, on the contrary, it was a sort of philanthropic era when whites, with generosity as their only motive, distributed pills and quinine to savages racked by fever.

The truth lies somewhere between these two interpretations. To impose their advanced technology on these peoples, the French, English and Belgians were often compelled to use force. In the Ivory Coast, for instance, it was long necessary to surround entire villages with troops in order to force the inhabitants to be vaccinated. They feared doctors and pills till well after the First World War. These unavoidable measures inevitably multiplied the vexations on both sides. Exhausted by incessant and often unrewarding and unrewarded work, many of the colonists lapsed into a habit of treating harshly the very natives they hoped by such admirable devotion to lead out of barbarism. And such is human nature that the brutalities left more lasting memories than the benefits that accompanied them, particularly among the educated Negroes who were imbued with the culture and moral values of the European.

From its first days, colonialism was caught in a tragic circle. To civilize the Africans it had to constrain them. And it was inevitable that the first natives to become the equals of their teachers would suffer that much more intensely the humiliations inflicted on their brothers. In a century free from revolutionary agitation, this resentment might have been tamped down, even overcome, by the material well-being engendered by economic development of the various colonies. But Communist demagoguery fore-stalled this outcome. In any case, the direct cause of the rising of the continent is to be found in this psychological reaction.

It might not even then have reached such vast dimen-sions if the local populations had been angered only by the faults of their respective colonial powers. But simultaneous with mounting their attacks on the French, the British and the Belgians, the young native elites made a discovery at once more general and painful and upsetting: the history they learned in European schools revealed to them that they belonged to one of the most despised of the human races. Before Stanley's arrival in the Congo, the natives had no means of knowing that the entire world had always looked to Africa for its slaves. To be sure, they had long suffered at the hands of slavers, but they considered this a localized calamity. The introduction of more advanced studies in Africa opened the eyes of the second generation of colonized Africans. With pain, and with rage, they rec-ognized that they shared with the Jews the fate of being the two most persecuted peoples on this planet. From an-cient Rome to the beginnings of the twentieth century, a sort of universal accord had condemned them to slavery. Christians and Moslems, Arabs and Berbers, Europeans and Americans had all in turn made use of them for servile manual labor.

The consciousness of this ancient wrong gave a collective significance to each individual offense perpetrated by the colonists. This transference of blame induced an immense traumatism which sustains the agitation in Africa today. Patrice Lumumba, speaking in front of King Baudouin at the independence celebrations in Léopoldville on June 30, 1961, flashed out: "We have known the sarcasm, the insults, the blows which we have had to suffer morning, noon and night because we were Negroes. . . ." Lumumba, a former trusted employee in the white administration, a commercial director of a European brewery with a good salary, had certainly never himself suffered the miseries he described with inflammatory eloquence. But his personal life was less important than the public anger he knew so well how to express. Men wiser by far than he have given vent to similar feelings. Speaking to an educated audience in France on October 2, 1959, Léopold Senghor, president of the Republic of Senegal, declared that in his opinion the relations between the rest of the world and his compatriots had long been characterized by "scorn for the Negro." Senghor, unlike Lumumba, was never a hate-filled demagogue; it is therefore important to heed his words, especially when he shows to what an impasse the humiliations suffered by his race could lead: "The revolt was purely negative, I confess it. The Negro students, of whom I was one in the years 1930-1934, were negativists. I confess we were racists. We were delirious in our *négritude*. No dialogue was then possible with Europe."

At a conference on "The Contribution of Religions to the Expression of the African Personality," held at Abidjan April 5, 1961, the young Ivory Coast writer, Bernard Dadié, commented brilliantly on the "delirium" Senghor had mentioned:

The desire *to be* gave birth to the theory of negritude: this negritude, which has caused so much ink to flow, was stirred in us by the frustration of being deprived in the course of history of the joy of creating and of being regarded at our real value. Negritude is nothing but our humble and tenacious ambition to rehabilitate the victims and to demonstrate to the world what has been specifically denied up to this time: the dignity of the Black Race.

This statement contains the basic, primordial objective of all political leaders in Africa from Nkrumah in Ghana to Jomo Kenyatta in Kenya. It expresses the reaction of the entire continent against its historic past. More important to the Negro than present day equality with other peoples is his desire for historical rehabilitation of his ancestors and their African cultures. Unhappily this demand has come in a universe dominated by technical developments. Africa has yet to participate in the progress of modern science; she is unlikely to do so in the immediate future. Her pretensions, however legitimate morally, are cruelly diminished by her weakness in material things. And this impotence, depending on the man and the country, is transformed either into fury or into self-deception. And all African leaders consider it an injustice. They have no intention of being regarded ever again as an "inferior" race now that they have, at long last, secured a theoretical right to equality. This stance propels them toward the two great myths of our time: African unity and the solidarity of all peoples of color.

Each of these formulas is a refuge against the unquestioned superiority of the European powers and of the United States. To counter the tons of steel poured every day in Europe and the United States, the Africans have nothing but their numbers. What the rulers of Dakar, Accra and Nairobi have been asking all along is not the emancipation of a particular tribe but the emancipation of the entire Negro race. Their consciousness of color in relation to the colonial domination has always been more important to them than their grievances against any particular country. The African nationalists have realized all along that they were lumped together by the outside world as Negroes, and this has mattered more to them than national identity as Guineans, Senegalese, Nigerians or Upper Volta-ites. How else could they feel when Guinea, the Senegal, Nigeria and Upper Volta were, until 1956, noth-

ing but administrative units, cut up or spliced together
according to the mood of their various conquerors?

By 1960, to be sure, the greater number of these territories had become independent republics. But none yet
possessed the ethnic, linguistic or territorial unity requisite
to the existence of a nation. At Dakar, the official radio
broadcasts in eight different dialects. The three and one
half million inhabitants of the Ivory Coast belong to sixty
tribes, many of them on unfriendly terms with each other.
Upper Volta was organized as a colony on March 1, 1919,
and made up of regions which had until then been part of
the Ivory Coast, Nigeria and the Sudan. Later, Upper
Volta was, by another stroke of the pen, broken up and the
various component elements returned to their countries
of origin. Finally, on September 4, 1947, it was definitively
reassembled. It would be possible to cite similar cases *ad
infinitum.* The point is that these continual shifts pre-
cluded the birth of any true national sentiments. The
moral revolt of the Negro people assumed the modern
form of a "nationalist" revolution. But it is, in fact, a
racial nationalism, a nationalism without nation.

The native elites understand this inner contradiction
perfectly. They dramatically exaggerate their weaknesses
vis-à-vis the great powers. And since, taken separately, none
of their nations has a real existence, they call themselves
and will themselves to be *Africans,* a designation they
proudly proclaimed at the Addis Ababa Conference (1963).
Thus they can not only continue their battle for the rehabilitation of the Negro race, but they are also persuaded
that the world will pay attention to the power of an entire
continent even as it refuses to acknowledge the power of
the individual nations on that continent.

The formation of the Afro-Asian group in the United
Nations has given powerful impetus to this tendency. Fol-

lowing their independence, India, Egypt, Indonesia, and their satellites had found themselves in a situation comparable to that of the Negroes. After the first flush of enthusiasm, Nasser, Nehru and Sukarno realistically assessed their weakness in resources compared to the great powers, and in particular compared to the power of the former colonial ruler. This common debility brought them together in a worldwide crusade against the colonial empires of France, Belgium, Holland and England. The goal of this political alliance was to reduce the material inferiority of each of the associated members through the formation of a diplomatic bloc capable of influencing world affairs. At the same time, the governments in New Delhi, Cairo and Jakarta encouraged revolts in Africa as another way to diminish the power of the traditional European colonial nations. This double strategy resulted in the Bandung Conference of 1955 where appeals were made which inflamed the ambitions of Negro leaders.

"Since the Renaissance, since the great discoveries that marked the start of the European colonization of the world, and particularly the colonization of the peoples of color, there has been no event of such historic importance," President Senghor would proclaim four years later. "The Bandung Conference was more than a military triumph that could establish a new political balance of power: it was more than a scientific discovery that might create new techniques and assure man's domination over his environment: *it was a moral victory of the colored peoples.*[1] These people, yesterday despised and dominated because they came from non-industrialized states, raised their heads for the first time and through the voices of their delegates proclaimed together their dignity as men. Aware that they represented the majority of humanity, they assumed the responsibility for their own well-being.

[1] Italicized in the text published in the magazine *Mali*, 1959.

They proclaimed the moral law that must govern relations between nations. . . . Bandung was more than that, as we shall see later. It was first of all the condemnation, before the bar of history, of *the fact of colonialism,* and through this of the white peoples of European origin, including the Russians."

While taking part in the conference which he was to talk about in such grandiloquent terms, the future president of Senegal was a secretary of state in the French Government of Edgar Faure! But it is as futile to point to this anomaly as to urge reasoned objections to the more exaggerated statements of this African leader. Objectively, it would certainly be possible to maintain that the arrival of Christopher Columbus in America was more important than the meeting of Chou En-lai with Nasser and Nehru. But Mr. Senghor's incantation is a response to an intense emotional drive. It rests on the mystical belief of the United Nations that it is enough to be "the majority of humanity" in order to rule the world; an abstraction confronts the concrete technical, military and economic superiority of the minority. Lacking material force, the Bandung nations fall back upon "morality" because there is no other road open to them; in point of fact it is a somewhat relative "morality," given India's actions against Kashmir, Communist China's against Tibet, Nasser's against Israel and Jordan, etc. But the black nationalists applaud because they find themselves in exactly the same position of weakness and bound by a terrible need to revenge themselves against "white peoples of European origin."

In this perspective, the leaders of the Afro-Asian group loomed as great men to Africans like Nkrumah, precisely because they had already taken action against Europe or against white peoples in general: Nasser had won against Britain in the Middle East; Chou En-lai headed a Red China that had been victorious over America in 1948 and over France at Dien Bien Phu in 1954; Sukarno was still aglow with his victories over the Dutch. But despite its progressive style and moral tinge, this was not a new phenomenon. In the first thirty years of the twentieth century, Asian nationalists and intellectuals had been enthusiastically pro-Japanese because Japan had crushed a European army in the Russo-Japanese war of 1904. In all fairness it should be pointed out that their enthusiasm for Japan was justified by exploits superior to those of the modern anticolonialists. To attain victory, the Empire of the Rising Sun had, since 1868, been building up its heavy industry and technical and scientific competence. At Port Arthur, the Czarist navy was attacked by a fleet built and armed by Japanese industry. What would Nasser do without his Soviet Migs? What would dozens of other underdeveloped countries do without their Russian or American arms?

In part because of this fundamental imbalance between its ambitions and its means, for a long time the myth of Bandung inflamed only a minority of Africans. While the nationalist militants were moved by the vivid expression of Senghor, the majority of the colonized peoples looked to the colonial power for amelioration of their lot. Paradoxically, the personal story of Léopold Senghor would seem to justify this hope. Senghor became the first Negro university fellow in the French language in 1935 and subsequently taught his own language to French children in a Paris lycée. In June 1940, when he was captured by the Germans he proved himself a courageous and unswerving French patriot. In 1946, he became a deputy in the French National Assembly and was among the authors of the Constitution of the Fourth Republic. The French Republic, from his youth to his present eminence, both encouraged and publicly recognized the successes of Mr. Senghor. His career was never hurt by the fact that he was a Negro. But there is no doubt that the future president of Senegal wanted at all times to maintain a feeling of solidarity with his less fortunate brothers, and the honors he received nourished in him no illusions about *their* daily lives.

As we have seen, colonialism developed complex and mixed human relations. An administrator would educate and take care of the children of a village while treating their parents harshly. Inevitably this attitude resulted in complex and mixed reactions on the part of the colonized. The intellectual, pampered by the whites, but emotionally involved with the most miserable of his own race, has a counterpart in another type of individual no less confused in his emotions: the African who was not understood by the Europeans but who believed sincerely in the benefits brought by Europe to his people. A few years ago, a minister of the Ivory Coast summed up this mixed reaction in a humorous quip: "I do not yearn for the good old days when, if a girl was pretty, one asked if it was before or after smallpox." Across Africa, millions of men echoed these sentiments. The civic tranquillity in Africa during the last war, its fidelity to the colonizing power, could only have resulted from such a feeling.

Just as nationalism has its adherents, so those who believe in continued adhesion to the mother countries have their theoreticians and defenders, notably Mr. Félix Houphouët-Boigny, founder of the first great political party in Africa and today president of the Ivory Coast.

In a famous speech in the great square of Abidjan in December, 1959, Mr. Houphouët-Boigny proclaimed: "I want to tell all those here assembled: don't be ashamed of having been colonized; all the peoples of the world have passed through a colonial stage; it is a universal condition. France was colonized; the United States also; there is no shame in having been colonized; it is a debt which one has paid. And colonialism, even for a fighter like me who has denounced all its abuses, was, if it was an evil, a necessary evil." Until 1960 the President of the Ivory Coast supported political federation between France and its African possessions and opposed the independence advocated by his adversary, Mr. Senghor. It was the opposition of General de Gaulle that doomed his project of federation. But before giving up, the unhappy premier made one last effort to explain his position to his compatriots. "The Ivory Coast has become independent," he told them, "because France has not accepted our proposal for federation. And it takes two to make a marriage—as I have often said before."

In Kwame Nkrumah, Jomo Kenyatta and Patrice Lumumba, the English and the Belgians met less friendly leaders. But in all areas, the tendency represented by Houphouët-Boigny had its advocates: Ronald Ngala in Kenya, Moise Tshombe in the Congo, the Ashanti tribes in Ghana. To beat down these forces it took the intervention of the Afro-Asian bloc, of the United Nations, of the USSR—and a policy split among the western powers.

Until the dispatch of United Nations troops to Léopoldville in July, 1960, the United Nations was happy to provide an international forum for Negro rebels, as they presented their cases against the colonizing powers. Every year petitioners left Togoland, the Cameroons, for New York to denounce the real and supposed abuses of France and England. Today, the Angolans are making the same pilgrimage to enter their complaints against Portugal and, as did their predecessors, getting the best reception from the Arabs and the Communists. In 1952, the Tunisians, at the instigation of their chief, Mr. Habib Bourguiba, inaugurated a particularly effective tactic. Through the intercession of the local government, then under a French protectorate, they asked the Security Council to arbitrate

their conflict with Paris. India, Russia and its satellites, Indonesia, Iraq and Pakistan approved this proposition, as
did the thirteen members of the Arab-Asiatic group. Between 1955 and 1962, the Algerian rebels were to adopt
this method with ever-increasing success. One would even
see their representatives (*i.e.*, rebels) seated among the *official* delegations of certain of the Moslem countries!

This diplomatic acclaim was of inestimable value to the
supporters of independence. It brought them allies
throughout the world and meant, in practice, that ambas-
sadors officially accredited to the United Nations took over
their propagandizing job. Without these diplomatic prece-
dents, the Yugoslav authorities might have hesitated to
smuggle arms to Algeria during the war. But why hold off
when with every new year a growing number of nations
find their place on the East River, each bringing a pledge
of help to the terrorists? This psychological pressure hampered the Europeans even in those regions of Africa where
there were no prospects of armed revolt. In their discus-
sions with the colonial administration, African leaders like
Lumumba and Kenyatta knew full well that they could
threaten to appeal to the United Nations as a final argument, and that such a threat was effective. The United
Nations, with its unfailing support of every exotic claim,
bears a direct responsibility for the upheavals in Africa
today. Its role, in degree and in kind, has grown greatly in
the last three years. Until 1960, it was content merely to
encourage anti-colonialism, but with the entry into that
body of twenty-odd Negro republics its orientation entered
a new phase. Today, the United Nations conducts and or-
ganizes the movement, whose consequences are, as a result,
greatly aggravated. These young African states exert no
influence on the larger areas of conflict, such as the German problem, the tensions between East and West, the
armaments race, etc. To provide themselves with an im-

portant role, they have launched a noisy crusade in favor of the Bantus of South Africa and the Portuguese colonial peoples. Success in these campaigns would help legitimize the national sovereignty of their instigators and would demonstrate their power. A defeat, conversely, would puncture their grandiose pretensions. The irresponsible battle being waged in Mozambique and Angola could well push the United Nations, and its committee on decolonization, into a dangerous adventure.

Such a policy cannot result in a satisfactory solution to the African crisis. If it succeeds, it will doubtless force the departure of the white masters and bring an end to racial conflict; but the experience of the Belgian Congo, of Algeria, proves that the eviction of the European solves nothing. Angola today, as the Congo the day before yesterday, and Algeria yesterday, is unified only by the European presence. In 1959, after a quarrel with his neighbor Nkrumah, President Houphouët-Boigny observed tellingly: "Just as there was no Ivory Coast before the arrival of Europeans in Africa, so there was no Gold Coast ⌈Ghana⌉. The Fanti, the Ashanti, the Zimba were never ought together before the arrival of the English. . . ." With the "centralizer" gone—be he French, Belgian, English, Portuguese—the tribes at once fling themselves at each other's throats to settle ancient quarrels that have been held in abeyance for fifty years. We saw this happen in Léopoldville, Elizabethville, Luluabourg, where unity was lost at independence. And these are not the exceptions, despite the relative stability of western Africa! The troubles of recent months in Dahomey, Senegal, the Congo (Brazzaville), in Chad, the Cameroons, the Ivory Coast, stem from ethnic pulls and jealousies. The United Nations has shown itself impotent in dealing with these complications. To be sure, its members were unanimous when it was a question of evicting the colonizer, but they were divided when it came to finding a replacement for him. We saw what happened in 1960 when it was necessary to choose between the fanaticism of Lumumba and the indolence of Kasavubu. The expensive United Nations military and civil mission in the Congo could not even arrive at a provisional remedy. After three years of international assistance, the Congo remained in a state of anarchy, and U Thant knew that when he pulled back his forces nothing had been altered.

Basically, the only power that stood to gain from this chaos in the Dark Continent was the Soviet Union with its revolutionary doctrines and experience. Despite this, the Communist entry into the battle for Africa was later and more maladroit than one would ever have imagined. French and Belgian Marxists had, of course, tried to exploit the unrest in Africa for the USSR, but these agents were known to the colonial administrators and they accomplished very little. The Soviet Union had no contiguous border with the African world, such as it had with Asia, or with the Middle East before 1917. Until 1960 only a handful of Soviet citizens had so much as set foot in such far-off countries as Nigeria, Upper Volta, Ubangi-Sha. The original plans for the subversion of Africa worked out in Moscow gave only a secondary role to the local inhabitants because of a very significant decision that had been made at the Fourth Congress of the International in 1922. The "Theses on the Negro Question," adopted at that time, came to totally ignorant conclusions: "History has given to the American Negro an important role in the freeing of the African peoples." Why this messianic role for the American Negro? Because the Communists believed that the main conflict would be "in America, as the center of Negro culture and the center of the crystallization of Negro protest." In strictly orthodox Marxist terms this error is easily explained. Obsessed by class-war theories, the Communists believed that the educated Negroes of the United States, more directly "exploited by capitalism" than the Negroes in the jungle, would revolt first. This erroneous calculation was spurred by the hope of seeing capitalism wounded at its very heart. Needless to say, facts have not borne out this hypothesis, but it does explain the Soviet Union's slow start in Africa.

Another phenomenon after the war, unhappily, mitigated the initial Soviet disadvantage in Africa. By sheer historical coincidence, the development of anti-colonialism on the Dark Continent emerged at the same time as the diffusion of Marxism on a worldwide scale. When Léopold Senghor started agitating for recognition of the dignity of the African in the years 1930-1934, Communism was more or less limited to certain circles in Europe and Asia. When Negro intellectuals talked of liberty at that period they quoted Voltaire and Jean-Jacques Rousseau. In the French territories, the concept of revolution itself was taught under a Third Republic that was in essence moderate, despite the ideology of 1789. In the British and Belgian possessions there were no liberation movements. In 1945 the entry of the Red Army into Berlin changed everything. An entire generation of future chiefs of state, from Sékou Touré to Modibo Keita, reached adulthood in a world astounded by Stalin's victories. The myth of 1917 suddenly eclipsed that of 1789. Lenin became a hero of greater stature than Lafayette or Danton. But above all the new doctrine gave the African revolt the magic formulas and incantations it needed to express itself in a modern idiom. The words, *exploitation, imperialism, socialism, colonialism,* so often used south of the Sahara in the last ten years were not forged between Dakar and Accra. They come directly from the Leninist repertory. Thanks to them, and despite its laggard start, the USSR had a good chance of penetrating Africa in a burst of anti-colonial agitation.

Its first attempts were hardly an unqualified success, however. As soon as Guinea achieved its independence, it opened wide its doors to Eastern "technicians" and "counselors." Hundreds of Czechs, Poles, Chinese and Russians fanned out through the continent, using Conakry as their entry point. This bridgehead seemed easy to exploit, since President Sékou Touré had been well-trained in Stalinism in the trade union movement before 1948. But, paradoxically, the very ease of the penetration worked against the Soviets. It encouraged them, in effect, to base their entire African policy on the alliance with Conakry. But to support Sékou Touré between 1958 and 1960 meant to quarrel with his neighbors and the republics of Equatorial Africa: The Ivory Coast, Senegal, Nigeria, Upper Volta, the Congo, Chad, etc. As long as she fulminated against "Colonialism," the Soviet Union was accorded a certain moral prestige by numerous intellectuals in these countries. But once the Russians started to support a regime in Conakry hostile to other governments, the Kremlin found itself dragged into purely African fights it could not control. Sékou Touré used the aid he was receiving from the Soviet Union to encourage subversion in the Cameroons, the Ivory Coast, and Senegal. The USSR seemed to be a partner in these enterprises. Many Negro leaders became convinced that the Communists were determined to overthrow them, personally. Despite the subsequent rupture between Conakry and Moscow, the Soviets are still suffering today, four years later, from this false start. Still, the very existence of the Soviet Union, which has divided the white race since 1917, is one of the profound causes of the uprisings of the colored peoples.

A second schism, that among the Western powers over Africa in the last few years, has compounded the grave consequences of the division existing since 1917. A major grievance against the United States in Europe today has to do with its intervention in the African affairs of France and of England. In July, 1957, when he was still only a young Senator from Massachusetts, John F. Kennedy came out publicly for Algerian independence. In the same year, after a trip to Ghana, Vice President Richard Nixon was to say: "The European powers in Africa, including Great Britain and France, carry the irrevocable stigma of their colonial past. The United States has no past of this sort in Africa. That is why it may become heir to the future in Africa." Did President Eisenhower's eminent collaborator know the exact nature and infinite complexity of the "stigma" in question? Did he ever meet with President Houphouët-Boigny, or men of his kind, as a counterpoise to his conversations with the hypernationalist Kwame Nkrumah? Like their Communist competitors, the Americans arrived late upon the scene in Africa. Until 1960 they had a number of consulates along the coasts, in capitals like Abidjan, Dakar and Accra. But they seldom ventured into the interior and knew little of the realities in the backwaters where "if a girl was pretty, one asked if it was before or after smallpox." Either through idealism, or in hopes of falling heir to the patrimony seen by Vice President Nixon, the United States has sustained anti-colonialism in the halls of the United Nations and throughout the world. It is consequently partly responsible for the troubles in the new Negro states.

But to dwell on this past serves little purpose, since what is done is done. Independent Africa is a reality today. Despite grave lacks, despite a disquieting instability in many countries, there are a number of wise leaders in Africa who recognize the dangers of Communism and are resolved to combat it. Mr. Houphouët-Boigny in the Ivory Coast, Mr. Senghor in Senegal, Mr. Ahidjo in the Cameroons, King Hassan II in Morocco, Mr. Abubakar Tafevva Belavva in

Nigeria. Certainly these men and their countries are faced today with thousands of problems. Beset by demagoguery, both internal and international, they may take the easy path without regard to the interests of the Free World. But the Free World must, nonetheless, choose its allies prudently and not, as it has so often in the past, scatter its support among nations that are hostile to each other. For example, it is not wise ostentatiously to help Ghana and Egypt when Nkrumah and Nasser are busy encouraging subversion in surrounding nations. By so doing, the Free World could well duplicate the mistake the Russians made in their support of Guinea. Above all the West should understand that it is to its advantage to encourage the formation of robust young nations whose health will form the best rampart against Communism. This policy calls for generous, but carefully supervised, economic aid; there is, in fact, no reason to support ostentatious spending for prestige's sake alone. This calls for agreement among the allies. In too many territories, the French, English, Belgians, Portuguese and Americans work under divergent orders, often one against the other. At the same time—and despite the Sino-Soviet conflict—the Marxists have demonstrated a relative unity of action.

If the disorders in Africa are to be mastered it must be by a global strategy. Nothing of importance will be accomplished so long as Washington, London and Paris do not agree on a common policy. To place our hopes for a solution in the United Nations would be, as the Congo has so graphically demonstrated, an expensive and disappointing waste of time.

Translated from the French by Priscilla L. Buckley.

3 African Political Economy

P. T. BAUER

PETER THOMAS BAUER *is Professor of Economics (with special reference to economic development and underdeveloped countries) at the London School of Economics. Born in 1915, he was educated at Scholae Piae, Budapest, and at Gonville and Caius College, Cambridge. He was formerly a Fellow of Gonville and Caius College and Smuts Reader in Commonwealth Studies at Cambridge University.*

Professor Bauer is the author of The Rubber Industry *(1948),* West African Trade *(1954),* The Economics of Underdeveloped Countries *(with B. S. Yamey, 1957),* Economic Analysis and Policy in Underdeveloped Countries *(1958), and* Indian Economic Policy and Development *(1961). He has also written many articles on economic subjects.*

I shall discuss in this essay certain aspects of African* economic development since the end of the nineteenth century; some prevalent ideas on economic development and some issues of policy. Africa is both vast and diverse, not

* Unless the contrary is indicated, I refer, in accordance with frequent usage, to Africa south of the Sahara. Most of the argument, however, would not be affected substantially if the continent as a whole were considered.

only in climate and physical resources and features, but, what is more relevant, in the level of economic attainment and rate of progress in the attitudes, customs, institutions and forms of government of its many peoples. The treatment is therefore necessarily highly selective. My main concern will be with a highly influential ideology which dominates public discussion of development in Africa, as in the world generally, and has far-reaching effects on policy. I shall examine this ideology and confront it with the actual situation in Africa; and I shall also examine the wider implications of the policy proposals that stem from it. I believe that the ideas are in contradiction to readily observable empirical evidence, and the policy proposals both impede material progress and create acute political tension.

I

The ideology is familiar in the writings emanating from the United Nations and its various specialist agencies, from members and associates of the Center of International Studies of M.I.T., and such well-known economists as Professor Gunnar Myrdal, Dr. H. W. Singer and others. Its main elements are these: underdeveloped countries are caught in a vicious circle of poverty and stagnation because their poverty prevents the accumulation of capital necessary for economic progress. This is intensified by the presence of rich countries whose mere existence obstructs in various ways the progress of the underdeveloped world, notably, but not only, by encouraging consumer spending in underdeveloped countries (who know about higher living standards elsewhere) and thereby discouraging such little saving and investment as might otherwise take place. The level of economic attainment and the rate of progress in Africa, as elsewhere, depends on government action (including inaction), which therefore also explains personal, regional, and international differences in income. The progress which might have taken place in Africa was repressed by the colonial system, under which the colonial governments not only failed to promote economic development, especially industrialization, but actually obstructed it and exploited the Africans.

The major policy implications are: an insistence on comprehensive development planning, that is, government determination of the composition and direction of economic activity outside the subsistence sector; compulsory saving, that is, massive taxation to finance government development projects; large-scale state support or ownership of manufacturing industry, the development of which is regarded as a condition of economic advance.

These general ideas and proposals are often supplemented by suggestions that, in order to attain and preserve economic as well as political independence, external economic relations must be substantially restricted and closely controlled, since they can obstruct economic progress and enhance the difficulties of national economic planning. National measures have to be supplemented by foreign aid, large-scale government-to-government grants or subsidized loans from abroad, since these countries are too poor to raise sufficient capital. The grant of aid is held to be politically in the interests of the donors, especially the United States, as otherwise the ever-widening international inequality of income would lead to political disaster. Moreover, massive foreign aid is a moral obligation on developed countries in view of their riches, and also to some extent in view of their responsibility for the poverty of underdeveloped countries, the latter consideration applying chiefly, but not only, to the former colonial powers.

The vicious circle of poverty and the axiomatic necessity for comprehensive development planning are the staple material of this ideology. In discussing it I shall quote from Professor Gunnar Myrdal,[1] formerly executive secretary of the United Nations Economic Commission for Europe, and one of the most explicit, emphatic, articulate and influential writers in this field:

It is the richer countries that are advancing while the poorer ones with the large populations are stagnating. For mankind as a whole there has actually been no progress at all . . .[2]

His policy proposals are epitomized in the following passages which deserve to be quoted at length:

It is now commonly agreed that an underdeveloped country should have a national economic development policy. Indeed, it should have an overall, integrated national plan, as is also urged by everybody. All underdeveloped countries are now, under the encouraging and congratulating applauses of the advanced countries, attempting to furnish themselves with such a plan—except a few that have not yet been reached by "the great awakening."

It is assumed by all that it is the national state which must be responsible for the overall plan and, indeed, for its initiation and pursuance. From one point of view, the plan is a program for the strategy of a national government in applying a system of state interferences in the play of the forces in the

---

[1] From two of his books: *Development and Underdevelopment* (Cairo, 1956), the published version of a series of lectures delivered in Cairo, that is, on African soil; and from *An International Economy* (London and New York, 1956), his most comprehensive work in this field.

[2] *An International Economy*, pp. 1-2. This is derived from Mr. H. W. Singer. Professor Myrdal writes: "As Mr. H. W. Singer has rightly pointed out, world real income per capita and with it the standard of living of the *average* human being, is probably lower than 25 years ago, and perhaps lower than in 1900, because the nations that have rapidly raised their economic standards have been a shrinking proportion of the total world population." (p. 2) The relevant passage in Mr. Singer's article, quoted verbatim in *An International Economy*, p. 341, reads: "If we define the average world income as that of the median world citizen the spectacular improvement which has occurred at one extreme and which has fascinated economists and other observers, becomes irrelevant." Apart from the absence or the severe limitations of statistics of income, these passages rest on a misleading and unwarranted use of the concept of average.

markets, thereby conditioning them and giving a push up-
wards to the social process which had settled down in a vicious
circle of inequality and economic regression, stagnation or a
too slow development.

What we witness is how this much more than half of mankind living in poverty and distress is not only accepting for itself
the pursuance on a grand scale of a policy line which we are
accustomed to call "socialistic," but that positive and urgent
advice to do so is given to them by all scholars and statesmen
in the advanced countries and by their governments when
participating in solemn resolutions of all the inter-govern-
mental organizations. Apparently nobody in the advanced
countries sees any other way out of the difficulties, which are
mounting in the underdeveloped countries, than the socialistic
one, however differently one's attitudes may be towards the
economic problems at home.[3]

Elsewhere he writes:

The special advisers to underdeveloped countries who have
taken the time and trouble to acquaint themselves with the
problem, no matter who they are . . . all recommend central
planning as the first condition of progress.[4]

and again:

However difficult the task, one thing stands out: the hope for
economic development for underdeveloped countries depends
very much on the State's being able to plan and to direct and
even to invest and to produce.[5]

The suggestion that for mankind as a whole there has
been no material progress is either meaningless rhetoric
or untrue. The statement that everyone in the developed
countries agrees that socialism is the only way out for the
underdeveloped countries is manifestly untrue, as there
are many prominent economists who do not accept this

[3] *Development and Underdevelopment*, p. 63.
[4] *An International Economy*, p. 201.
[5] *Ibid.*, p. 210.

view. Professor Myrdal is, however, right that advisers to
underdeveloped countries generally recommend central
planning. This is because subscribers to the dominant ideology are appointed as advisers. But this indicates only the
method of selection and not the consensus of economists.

II

There exists another very different literature on African
development; beginning about 1900, anthropologists, historians, economists and others have discussed the rapid
change in Africa since the end of the nineteenth century
and the problems associated with it. Although much of it
is authoritative, it figures little in present-day public discussion. The major emphasis is on the problems and
dilemmas of rapid change: the difficulties of adapting institutions and attitudes to fast-changing conditions; the
transition from communal to individual tenure of land;
the results of detribalization and disintegration of communal life and values; and the difficulties of rapid urbani-
zation.

Examples of this literature include writings by Mary
Kingsley, Margery Perham, Professor S. Herbert Frankel,
Lord Hailey, Sir Keith Hancock, F. J. Pedler, among many
others. I shall quote from it at some length as it is little
known to non-specialists and because it presents a picture
of Africa very different from that usually envisaged.

Mary Kingsley [6] was an early writer of this school. She
wrote on the impact of the culture of nineteenth-century
Europe on the African whose outlook was that of much
earlier cultures. Here is a typical passage:

If you will try science [*i.e.* anthropology] all the evils of the
clash between two culture periods could be avoided, and you

6 *West African Studies* (London, 1901), and *Travels in West Africa*
(London, 1904).

could assist these West Africans in their thirteenth-century
state to rise into their nineteenth-century state without having
the hard fight for it which you have had. . . . There is absolutely no perceivable reason why you should not do it if you
will try science, and master the knowledge of the Native and
his country.[7]

In 1926, well before African development became a
major international issue, Dr. A. McPhee published a book
with the revealing title: *The Economic Revolution in
British West Africa.*[8] The following passages epitomize his
conclusions:

In fact, the process since the 'Nineties of last century has been
the superimposition of the twentieth century after Christ on
the twentieth century before Christ, and a large part of the
problem of native policy is concerned with the clash of such
widely different cultures and with the protection of the natives
during the difficulties of transition.

The transition has been from the growth of subsistence crops
and the collection of sylvan produce to the cultivation of exchange crops, with the necessary implication of a transition
from a "Natural" economy to a "Monetary" economy, and the
innumerable important reactions from the latter phase.[9]

Sir Keith Hancock, judicious and critical historian of
African development, discusses this at some length in his
Survey of British Commonwealth Affairs. Here are some
of his observations on the changes in West Africa over the
previous half-century:

In some periods of European history—in our own day, for
example, or in the day of the first steam-engines and power
mills—the European world has seemed to be transformed; Europe nevertheless has remained the same world, spinning

7 *West African Studies,* pp. 326-27. Quoted in Sir Keith Hancock, *Survey
of British Commonwealth Affairs* (London, 1942), Vol. II, Part 2, p. 333.
   8 London, 1926.
   9 P. 8. The author points out that similar changes were occurring in
East Africa and quotes an interesting government report to support this.

very much faster. But in Africa change means more than ac-
celeration. Europe's commerce and its money-measurements
really have brought the African into a new world. Its economics are different from his "primitive economics"; its personal relationships have nothing to do with his relationships
of matrilineal families and tribal kinship. His religion does
not in any way reinforce or govern the capitalism into which
he has been swept. He retains something of his old social and
religious and mental life and habit—these things are very
slow in dying—but they are distinct from his new economic
life and habit.[10]

These writers were not apologists for the government or
private enterprise, nor were they sentimentalists deplor-
ing the changes which were taking place. Mostly, they
regarded the changes as inevitable and, on balance, beneficial, and they wished to see the advance accelerated, but
in a manner which would minimize its strains and hard-
ships.

The baffling dilemmas presented to governments by the
impact of rapid change were particularly evident in the
context of land tenure, notably whether individual rights
in the cultivation and ownership of land should be permitted to replace communal or tribal tenure wholly or in
part, a problem which would not arise in a static or stag-
nant society. According to Professor Frankel, one of the
most knowledgeable and penetrating observers of the African scene, well-meant but mistaken decisions in this field
taken before the First World War have had far-reaching
consequences in East and South Africa, retarding the more
secure advances of the Africans in East Africa and leading
South African policy into its present impasse. He writes
in a recently published and closely argued paper:

Looking back from the vantage point of our own times, it
is clear that the root cause of the economic backwardness of

10 Vol. II, Part 2, p. 283.

various African territories as well as of the Native areas in the Union lies in the failure to modify customary control of land occupation and tenure, which has prevented the emergence of land use and ownership compatible with modern forms of commercialized production in a money economy. The failure to make of the land a viable economic factor of production has condemned the peoples on it to eke out a precarious subsistence. . . . As long as communal systems of land tenure and the ban on Native purchase of land in European areas continued, those able and willing to embark upon new methods of production were unable to obtain land holdings of suitable size, adequately protected against tribal rights and authority, and ensuring to the owner the undisturbed fruits of his labour for himself and his heirs. The enterprising, the unemployed, or the redundant were, therefore, condemned to wander to the towns or to other European areas to sell their labour.[11]

This was also the diagnosis of the East Africa Royal Commission, whose report was written at the height of the Mau-Mau crisis.[12] Passages and references which reflect the preoccupation with the problems of rapid and uneven change could be multiplied easily.

III

There has been very rapid material progress in many parts of Africa over the last sixty to eighty years, particularly in regions where the developed countries have established close contact. This disposes both of the vicious circle of poverty (the cornerstone of the dominant ideology) and of the allegation that contact with the developed world has obstructed African progress. This is, of course, not to say

[11] *The Tyranny of Economic Paternalism in Africa: A Study of Frontier Mentality 1860–1960* (Johannesburg, 1960), p. 7.

[12] *Report of the East Africa Royal Commission 1953–1955* (London, 1955); *e.g.*, pp. 8 and 9.

that people in the materially advanced parts are either more or less happy than they are elsewhere or than their forebears. But this is a different issue.

The experience of Ghana and Nigeria is especially noteworthy. These countries are in the forefront of current political developments in Africa; both were colonies until 1957 and 1960 respectively; appreciably over 99½ percent of their population is African, and there are and always have been only a handful of non-African civil servants and traders there. The rapid progress of these countries since the end of the nineteenth century is well brought out in foreign trade statistics. For various reasons these statistics are unusually reliable and they are also meaningful because all agricultural exports are produced by Africans, as there are no foreign-owned plantations there; the vast bulk of imports is destined for Africans, as the non-African population is numerically insignificant. Moreover, until recently there was either no, or only negligible, local production of the type of commodities imported, so that the imports indicate the total local consumption or use of these commodities.

Around 1900 total annual imports and exports of Nigeria were each about £2 million, while at present * they are each about £200 million; for Ghana (formerly the Gold Coast) the corresponding annual figures are about £1 million and £100 million. Over this period there has been a spectacular increase in imports of both consumer and capital goods into these territories. In 1900 there were no imports, or only negligible imports, into these territories of flour, sugar, cigarettes, cement, petroleum products or iron and

---

* For simplicity of exposition, it is the present position which is contrasted with that at the turn of the century. To forestall a possible objection that the origin of the progress is only recent, it might be stated explicitly that most of it occurred (in real, as disinct from money, terms) before the Second World War. This is shown in the cocoa statistics quoted later in this section.

steel. In recent years these have been on a massive scale, except when they have been replaced by local production, as in the case of cement and cigarettes. Exports of cocoa, groundnuts, or cotton from Nigeria or the Gold Coast were nil or negligible in 1900, while exports of oil palm produce from Nigeria were about one-tenth of their present volume. Today these are staple exports of world commerce, and annual shipments are hundreds of thousands of tons. To take but one example, in 1895 cocoa exports from the Gold Coast were about 34 tons; from Nigeria there were none. By the mid-1930's they were about 300,000 tons from the Gold Coast and about 80,000 tons from Nigeria; at present there are over 400,000 tons from Ghana and about 120,000 tons from Nigeria, all from holdings planted, operated and owned by Africans.

There is of course much other information on the material progress of these countries from sporadic estimates of the national income, and from such more reliable and meaningful statistics as those of education, public health, government revenue, transport and so on. In both countries (as elsewhere in Africa) the population has increased greatly as a result of the reduction in death rates which implies a substantial increase in life expectation. The population of what is now Ghana, for instance, has approximately trebled since 1900. The information about Nigeria is very scanty, but the population has certainly increased very greatly since 1900; it has probably more than doubled. Such statistics cannot convey the far-reaching and pervasive changes which have transformed life over large parts of West Africa. Slavery, slave raiding, communal disorder and famine have been largely eliminated; there has been a large reduction in endemic and epidemic disease and a substantial development of communications. At the turn of the century Kano in Northern Nigeria was still an important slave market; today it is the center of the groundnut industry.

None of this is intended in the least to suggest that all is, or was, for the best in these countries. Throughout this period there were considerable political and economic problems and difficulties. But it is to deprive words of their meaning to assert that these areas have experienced no material progress and are caught in a vicious circle of poverty and stagnation. Nor should the foregoing be interpreted as a plea for *laissez-faire* or any other particular policy. But it is obvious that the problems of rapid and uneven growth are radically different from those of stagnation and require a very different kind of official action.

The colonial status of these territories does not seem to have retarded their progress. Rather the reverse, as it promoted the inflow of administrative, commercial and technical skills as well as of capital which has helped to maintain law and order and promoted the far-reaching changes in West Africa. It was particularly necessary for the construction of railways and other communications, which were most expensive and difficult in West Africa. Dr. McPhee indicates some of these difficulties in describing the construction of the Gold Coast railway by the colonial government around 1900:

In considering the cost of the construction of railways in West Africa it is necessary to recollect that they have been constructed through dense tropical forest in what is generally recognised as the worst climate in the world, necessitating very short hours of service and constant changes of staff in every grade: with very heavy rainfall: with scarcity and inferiority of unskilled labour: with considerable landing difficulties: and the necessity of carrying on construction entirely from one base, owing to absence of roads or paths of any description to facilitate the transport of materials in advance of the railhead. Further allowance must be made for the native revolts and military operations which have occurred in each case, causing interruptions and disorganisation. . . . Another factor making for high costs was the scarcity of ballast in most parts.[13]

There is in West Africa an independent country, Liberia, the material progress of which was far slower; indeed, in comparison with Ghana and Nigeria it was barely perceptible over this period, which hardly suggests that African political independence has been more conducive to economic progress than has colonial status. This was explicitly and courteously, though somewhat unexpectedly, recognized by the representative of Liberia at the United Nations on the accession of Ghana to the United Nations as a sovereign state. He said: "The remarkable development of the state of Ghana while it was under guardianship provides a unique example of what can be accomplished through the processes of mutual cooperation and goodwill among peoples." [14]

The West African experience is only a most striking example of a more general experience in Africa. There has been substantial material advance in many parts of the continent since the turn of the century, generally starting from extremely primitive and indeed savage conditions; in every case it has occurred in areas and among people in established contact with the developed world; the colonial status has promoted rather than retarded this advance (the position of two African countries, Ethiopia and Liberia, that have been completely independent throughout and that are neighbors of colonial areas, tends to bear this out). And at present, throughout the region, the most prosperous areas and sectors are those in contact with the developed world, notably the crop-producing areas and the ports of West Africa, the European-settler region of East Africa, and the mineral-producing areas of Central and

13 *The Economic Revolution in British West Africa*, p. 112.
14 Speech at the United Nations General Assembly, March 8, 1957.

South Africa; conversely, the poorest and most backward are those populations with few or no external contacts.

The material advance of many African territories, then, flatly contradicts the thesis of the vicious circle of poverty and stagnation. This is, of course, refuted also by the very existence of developed countries, all of which began as underdeveloped; indeed, it is refuted by the very notion of development. More generally, the thesis is contradicted by the rise from poverty to riches of innumerable individuals and groups throughout the world in both developed and underdeveloped countries: this would be impossible if there existed a practically insurmountable vicious circle of poverty. It is indeed remarkable that this thesis should have been so widely publicized and accepted when it is in flagrant contradiction to simple logic and obvious empirical evidence.

IV

Africa is still very poor by comparison to Europe, North America and other developed regions, though not quite as poor as conventional comparisons suggest, which, for various reasons, very greatly exaggerate the international differences in income. The most up-to-date and systematic discussion, both of the extent of the exaggeration of the conventional comparisons and the reason for it, is to be found in articles by Dr. D. Usher. In his article "The Transport Bias in Comparisons of National Income," he writes:

For example, the conventional comparison shows that the *per capita* national income of the United Kingdom is about fourteen times that of Thailand. Recomputations made by the author to allow for various biases in the comparison suggest that the effective ratio of living standards is about three to one. Even if the recomputed ratio is doubled, the change in order of magnitude is large enough to affect our way of thinking about the underdeveloped countries.[15]

But poverty is compatible even with rapid advance, if this has begun only recently and has started from a very low level, which is the situation in Africa. Sub-Saharan Africa especially was materially extremely backward in the nineteenth century, almost unimaginably so by Western standards. Although the tribal societies had internal cohesion and order, the people were extremely poor—subsistence producers depending on a very harsh nature. Apart from slave trading and raiding there was until the third quarter of the nineteenth century practically no contact between the interior of Africa and the outside world, and very little between different parts of Africa, even between areas comparatively close to each other (apart from the caravan routes of the Sahara where in the eighteenth and nineteenth centuries slave traffic was prominent). Various natural features (still present) made access to the interior and communications within it extremely difficult. Before the advent of the Europeans there were neither railways nor roads in sub-Saharan Africa. There were only primitive paths, some of them cut during the periodic visits of Arab traders in slaves and ivory, some jungle tracks which were often only animal trails. There was, therefore, very little communication between the different indigenous tribes. This isolation of different areas over a very long period no doubt contributed to the multiplicity of distinct tribes and languages in many parts of Africa. In Liberia, with an estimated population of around one and a half million, there are about twenty different languages.

Human porterage, which is extremely expensive, when practical at all, severely limited transport in distance and

15 *Economica*, May, 1963, p. 140.

bulk. In 1900 there were 32 miles of railway in British West Africa and none at all in British East Africa. By 1950 there were about 3,000 miles of railway in each. This is a modest mileage for such large areas with substantial population, but it signifies some achievement considering that construction not only started from scratch, but was also very expensive in view of the great technical and economic problems. The first East African railway, the Kenya-Uganda railway, had to be built entirely by Indian labor especially imported for this purpose. There were also thousands of miles of roads built in both East and West Africa over this period, whereas in 1900 there were hardly any roads in West Africa and none at all in East Africa.

Recognition of these easily verifiable facts should help place in perspective the allegation that European influence or the colonial governments are responsible for the fragmentation of Africa, that they have "Balkanized" the continent and unnaturally separated one African nation from another. Kwame Nkrumah, for example, states: "Many of them have deliberately been made so weak economically, by being carved up into many separate countries, that they are not able to sustain out of their own resources the machinery of independent government." [16]

Outside a handful of mission schools there were absolutely no schools in sub-Saharan Africa at the end of the nineteenth century. Children were, of course, introduced to the skills, customs and duties required for tribal life. But there was no schooling or education in the accepted sense of the word, as there is none today in the areas not in contact with Europeans. Many picturesque examples could be given of the conditions in Africa at the end of the nineteenth century. In 1895 the headquarters of the Royal Niger Company was successfully attacked by African

[16] *Africa Must Unite* (London, 1963), p. 184. The book appears in a series entitled Heinemann Educational Books.

tribesmen, who abducted forty-three of that company's African employees for a cannibal feast. This was actually quite near the coast. Barbarous customs of great antiquity cannot be eradicated within a few decades. In the 1940's there still were instances of ritual murder and of cannibalism in West Africa. The progess of the last half-century must be seen against this background.

V

The establishment and rapid expansion since about 1900 of the production of cash crops by Africans, usually on small properties but on a massive scale in the aggregate, mostly but not only for export, is a significant feature of the African scene. It has been a principal instrument of the economic advance of the African populations of West Africa and East Africa. The main crops are cocoa, groundnuts, coffee, kola nuts and cotton; less important products include, among others, rubber, maize and tobacco. Palm oil and palm kernels are quantitatively very important exports produced by Africans and they have increased greatly in this century. Their production, however, is derived from naturally occurring trees, not from holdings especially planted for the purpose. In American language groundnuts are peanuts. But they are not "just peanuts." They are a leading oilseed, a major source of edible oils and food and cattle feed. The kola nut (unrelated to Coca Cola) is a versatile tree crop of West Africa. It serves as a concentrated food, a stimulant, a cosmetic agent and a gift for ceremonial occasions. It is a major article of the internal trade of West Africa. Cocoa cultivation in the Gold Coast began in the 1890's; the cultivation of the other cash crops appreciably later.

This rapid and massive expansion has a number of very interesting implications.

First, the phenomenal expansion of these African-produced crops from a zero or negligible amount to leading staples of world commerce within a few decades conclusively disposes of the suggestion that Africans do not respond to economic incentives or cannot produce competitively for the world markets.

Second, the establishment of these holdings by Africans represents massive direct investment in agriculture, which is important in many parts of the world and is very often ignored in estimates of capital formation. This type of investment is yet another refutation of the argument that poverty precludes economic advance.

Third, it shows that a rapid and comparatively smooth progress is possible in Africa without industrialization. The comparative smoothness of advance through the production of cash crops is not surprising, since it involves less of a break with traditional pursuits and ways of living than does large-scale manufacturing or mining. The unavoidable difficulties of adjustment involved in progress from subsistence production to production for wider exchange and sale are not accentuated by violent changes in the pattern of life and by the additional need of rapidly acquiring knowledge of unfamiliar techniques. The comparative smoothness of the advance is also shown by the fact that the establishment of the kola nut industry, now a large scale activity in Western Nigeria, passed unnoticed until years after it had become quantitatively important (which was reflected in railway returns, among other pieces of evidence).

Fourth, this investment also refutes the notion that individual Africans are invariably unenterprising and cannot become entrepreneurs. The massive production of cash export crops is a particularly obvious refutation of this notion, which is also contradicted by the activities of African traders.

Fifth, and this is of particular interest, this development conclusively refutes the suggestion that the African cannot take a long-term view, an opinion well known to anthropologists to be erroneous. Many of these crops, especially cocoa, kola nuts and coffee, are the products of planted trees or bushes which reach maturity only several years after planting. (Coffee four years, and cocoa and kola nuts five years at the earliest.) Thus anyone planting these crops looks forward for a long period. This effectively disproves two opinions influentially canvassed in widely different quarters: one, that the African is a child of nature living for the present and giving no thought for the morrow; the other, that private individuals in underdeveloped countries, especially in Africa, do not take the long view required for progressive investment decisions, so that these must be transferred to the government.

VI

A widely canvassed objection to the foregoing reasoning and evidence needs to be considered. This is that the advancing sectors in underdeveloped countries, particularly in Africa, are enclaves carved out of the local economies by the advanced countries, outposts of advanced economies which do not serve to improve the economic position or prospects of the local population.[17] The suggestion that they do not benefit the local population is demonstrably untrue. For instance, all agricultural exports from West Africa and Uganda are produced entirely by Africans on their own lands. Africans also have a large share in the transport, distribution and simple processing of these exports as well as in the distribution of imports. Even where enterprises in the advanced sectors are foreign, they

[17] Numerous references can be cited; for instance, Professor Myrdal, *An International Economy*, pp. 100-2 and 107.

normally still assist development by contributing to government revenues, by spreading skills and generally promoting the exchange economy. These sectors are not enclaves cut off from the rest of the economy, but the points of first impact of development. Economic advance always affects certain regions and activities first, from which it spreads outwards. The time this requires depends, among other factors, on the qualities of the population, on customs and attitudes, on institutional factors and physical communications. The term "enclave" is also very misleading in this general context as it suggests the carving out or even removal of something which existed previously. In fact, economic activities and assets to which this term refers were introduced and developed by external resources, usually from scratch or nearly so, but often in cooperation with local resources.

All African countries are poor; the incomes earned by Africans throughout Africa are low; apart from European-owned mines, estates and trading companies, small scale agriculture is the main economic activity; in the advanced sectors, foreign personnel, enterprise and capital are prominent; and foreigners working in these sectors normally earn high incomes compared to the local population (this reflects, of course, their command over skills and capital which could earn relatively high incomes in developed countries). Many writers, notably Professor Myrdal and President Nkrumah, refer to such economies as colonial economies, and they include the economies of independent sovereign countries whose policies are not controlled by other governments. This usage quite simply identifies poverty with colonialism, and thereby deprives the latter term of all meaning. President Nkrumah sees in economic colonialism, or neo-colonialism, a great danger to African countries, but he does not make clear what he means by these terms.

Although the term "neo-colonialism" or economic colonialism is quite meaningless, it has gained wide acceptance. Its popularity reflects in turn certain ideas and political factors which are worth noting because of both their intellectual and political influence. They include the belief that economic development generally and the development of manufacturing industry in particular (which is axiomatically regarded as an instrument of progress without discussing its costs) depend on government action, so that poverty, especially if it is accompanied by lack of industrialization, reflects failure of the government to act appropriately. Similarly, international differences in economic attainment and rates of progress (including differences in incomes locally between foreigners and members of the local population) are considered abnormal and reprehensible, the results of past or present pressures from abroad. Thus the poverty in the politically independent African countries is regarded as the result either of past colonial domination or of still operative external factors or both, *i.e.* of colonialism, past or present. In fact, throughout Africa, as elsewhere in the underdeveloped world, the most advanced sectors are those in contact with the outside world. In both independent countries and colonies the most backward are those untouched by external contacts, with the aborigines being the limiting case. This is but one obvious refutation of the argument that external forces are responsible for African poverty.

VII

According to the dominant ideology economic attainment depends on government policy; and insistence on government planning as the necessary and apparently sufficient condition of progress is its central tenet. In prescription as in diagnosis, Professor Myrdal is probably the most explicit and influential exponent of the ideology with his emphatic insistence on government planning as the determinant of economic progress. Such factors as climate, natural resources, economic qualities, customs and attitudes do not figure either in his diagnosis or his proposals. "The political independence they have won for themselves, or are now winning," he says, "is their most precious asset: the national state." [18] If sovereign status were so important for economic advance it is difficult to see why there are, and always have been, so many very poor independent countries in the world, including those in Africa: Ethiopia, independent since time immemorial, much longer than many developed countries (including the United States), and Liberia, independent at least since 1847, are among the materially most backward countries in Africa, perhaps the most backward. Professor Myrdal simply asserts that economic attainment depends largely on government action and that the government of an independent country will be both able and willing to promote economic development, without explaining why.

The dominant ideology interprets central planning not simply as the phasing or coordination of public investment, but as comprehensive and detailed control over the economy. Professor Myrdal writes:

A main element of every national development plan is a decision to increase the total amount of investment, aimed at raising the productive powers of the country, and to procure the capital formation necessary for this purpose. The plan must determine this overall amount and must, in addition, determine the proportions of the capital which should be allocated in different directions: to increase the overall facilities in transport and power production; to construct new plants and acquire the machinery for heavy industries and for light industries of various types; to raise the productivity level in

18 *Development and Underdevelopment*, p. 59.

agriculture by long-term investments in irrigation schemes and short term investments in tools, machinery and fertilizers; to improve the levels of health, education and training of the working people, and so on. To be practical and effective, the plan must be worked out not only as a general frame but must have this frame filled and concretized by careful segmental planning. And it must contain definite direction on all points and, in addition, spell out instructions for the specific inducements and controls by which the realisation of those directives becomes effected.[19]

Comprehensive development planning thus means that what is produced is determined largely by the government rather than by the individuals comprising the society. To quote again from Professor Myrdal:

The national plans cannot be made in terms of costs and profits for the individual enterprises; they can, in fact, not be made in terms of the prices in the markets . . . the whole meaning of the national plan is to give such shelter from market forces to investment, enterprise and production that they become undertaken in spite of the fact that they are not remunerative according to private business calculations.

It is here that the national state comes in as representing the common and long-term interests of the community at large. It senses the fictitiousness of the private business calculations in terms of costs and profits. . . .

The plan and its targets, in other words, have to render the basis for deciding the criteria: the decisions themselves are political decisions reached in terms of national welfare as this is determined by the political process.[20]

This certainly does not show how the economy is to benefit from the overriding of the decisions of the individuals comprising it. It assumes axiomatically that the economy will progress more rapidly if what is produced is deter-

[19] *Ibid.*, pp. 63-64.
[20] *Ibid.*, pp. 66-67. (Italic in original)

mined largely by the government rather than by individual consumers and producers. Such a policy does not augment resources but only centralizes power. Not one of the now developed countries resorted to comprehensive planning in the past. Nor is it used in Hong Kong, the underdeveloped country which has progressed most strikingly in recent years.

VIII

Statements such as Professor Myrdal's, which could be multiplied, take the case for comprehensive planning for granted without argument. But it is by no means obvious why an economy should progress more rapidly if what is produced is determined largely by the government, rather than by individual consumers and producers. At times the advocacy of comprehensive planning is supported by arguments which seem to have specific content and some superficial plausibility, but they vanish on examination. One is that comprehensive planning is necessary to promote industrialization, particularly the development of heavy industry. In fact, there has been massive development of manufacturing in many developed and underdeveloped countries (the latter including Hong Kong, Japan and Brazil, among others) without such policies. There may well be all sorts of activities which would not emerge without comprehensive planning, but it does not in the least follow that they would represent either an efficient use of resources or that they would promote the growth of resources. Counsel has often been darkened in this field by focussing attention on particular activities, regarding these somehow as a net addition to output, and disregarding not only the demand for the output, but also costs in terms of alternative use of resources. It is certainly not clear why and how the overriding of the decisions of individuals should increase the flow of income, especially the flow of desired goods and services which constitute the standard of living. The critical remarks in this paragraph and elsewhere in this section do not of course apply to the familiar instances of indiscriminate benefits yielded by traditional government activities and the capital expenditure associated with these. Indeed some of these activities, especially in the fields of public health and basic communications, can yield striking benefits in underdeveloped countries. But this is a different matter from comprehensive planning.

Again it is often said that government planning is required in poor countries because of a lack of entrepreneurial talent there. Quite apart from the manifest invalidity of this allegation in many African countries, the obvious question arises, where is the government going to get entrepreneurial talent if there is none in the country? Comprehensive planning is also sometimes advocated as necessary to increase investment expenditure. This is again irrelevant, since saving and investment can be encouraged by a budget surplus or by various measures encouraging private savings and investment. This is quite apart from the question that a piece of expenditure does not become productive by being labeled investment. The merits of an investment program cannot be assessed meaningfully, except in terms of some estimates of prospective returns against costs in terms of alternative uses of the resources, taking into account also the repercussions of both the collection and the expenditure of funds.

Once comprehensive planning is adopted and the case for it assumed axiomatically, then either stagnation or progress can be adduced in favor of its continuation and extension with superficial plausibility: stagnation of the economy can be adduced as evidence of the necessity for its extension, and progress as evidence of its success. On this basis there need be no limit, either to the continuation or to the extension of this policy. Myrdal puts it neatly: "When, as a matter of fact, many underdeveloped countries demonstrate shocking waste of very scarce resources in 'showpiece' public works and in subsidizing expensive starts of investment and production along blind alleys, this is the result of their failure to apply rigid planning, and the only cure is to improve their planning." [21]

There is one argument in the advocacy of comprehensive planning which is prominent in Africa and is therefore worthwhile considering in some detail. This is that central planning is necessary for economic independence. If this means only the enlargement of manufacturing industry or of some other activity or range of activities, there is no need to add much to what has already been said. In any case subsidization of one particular activity does not strengthen the economy. Nor do such policies serve usually to reduce the economic risks confronting a country as effectively as the building up of foreign-exchange reserves or the promotion of the flexibility of the economy by the improvement of communications or its system of education. But the advocates of economic independence may mean something more ambitious, though this is not easy to ascertain because the aim is imprecise. Political independence, in the sense of national sovereignty, is a clear-cut concept, namely, the freedom of the government to act without reference to external authority. By analogy, economic independence would seem to mean a state of affairs under which a country is unaffected by external economic conditions. But this implies the reduction of external contacts to an absolute minimum. And this, on the face of it, does not seem desirable in the sense of improving the economic conditions of its inhabitants. Economic independence, in the sense of absence of external contacts, is fully obtainable only by subsistence producers and, as is well

21 *Ibid.*, p. 69.

known, subsistence production is generally incompatible with even a tolerable level of economic attainment. It is no accident that throughout the underdeveloped world, and especially so in Africa, the most backward parts are those with the fewest external contacts.

What effects economic progress, in fact, is not economic independence, in the sense of self-sufficient isolation, but economic interdependence, in the sense of extensive external contacts. The importance of external economic contacts must be manifest. These are the channels through which human and material resources, skills and capital from developed countries, reach the underdeveloped world. They open up new markets and sources of supply, and they bring new commodities and techniques to the notice of the local population. They undermine the traditional customs and attitudes which obstruct material advance: they arouse expectations and dissatisfaction with existing circumstances, which is the first condition of economic progress.

These external contacts enabled the Africans to draw on the capital resources and technical skills of developed countries, which raised and maintained the African economies above subsistence production. At present these contacts offer exceptional opportunities. Because of the presence of advanced countries and highly developed communications, the underdeveloped world has readier access to the fruits of scientific and technical progress than the now developed countries had in the past. Access to this accumulated knowledge could be as helpful as access to unused land was to other countries in times past. The ability of the underdeveloped countries to take advantage of this depends greatly on the attitudes and skills of their own peoples, as well as on government policies promoting or restricting international contacts.

The advocacy of economic independence, in the sense of

minimal external contacts and even those under government control, stems from the desire for a closely controlled economy. As we have seen, central planning in the sense of government determination of the composition and direction of economic activity is influentially advocated and, again as already argued, it is not at all clear why and how this promotes a rise in general living standards. But it certainly promotes a concentration of power in the hands of the government, which the advocates of centrally controlled economies consider desirable; and reduction of external contacts usually facilitates government control of the economy.

IX

Throughout Africa, and especially in the former British territories, measures have been introduced during the last twenty or thirty years which established close government control over the economies of these countries. For instance, practically all agricultural exports produced by Africans have come to be covered by state export monopolies. As a result of these measures tightly controlled economies were created in which people's lives and activities and the alternatives open to them (aside from subsistence production) as producers, consumers and traders have come to be largely determined by the government. These measures include the establishment of state trading monopolies; extensive licensing of industrial and commercial activities; and the setting up of many government-owned and operated so-called cooperatives. The origins of these measures are diverse. They include a tradition of paternalism in many parts of Africa; more important, the pressure of sectional, political, administrative and economic interests; the desire of administrators to enlarge their powers; and at times the belief that a controlled economy is tidier and better organized than one without such controls.

The export monopolies over agricultural crops produced by Africans throughout the former British colonies are much the most significant of these controls. They cover such important crops as cocoa, groundnuts, palm oil, palm kernels, coffee, cotton and a number of others. This system was originally introduced under the pressure of sectional interests. For decades before the Second World War the West African export merchants introduced quasi-monopolistic, market-sharing agreements designed to restrain competition among themselves in the purchase of export production. They always broke down. In 1939, on the outbreak of war, they successfully prevailed on the British authorities in West Africa and Britain to give statutory power to these schemes. The administration of these statutory buying cartels was, however, easier when the ultimate purchaser (*i.e.* the organization buying the exports from the merchants) also had a monopoly, and the merchants therefore pressed for a statutory export monopoly as well as for statutory quotas in the purchase of the crops. This is the origin of the West African marketing boards, which were subsequently extended elsewhere in British Africa with far-reaching results. The system gives to the government-operated or controlled monopolies enormous power over the livelihood of the producers, besides serving as a powerful source of finance and patronage for the ruling party. Hundreds of millions of pounds sterling have been withheld from the producers in Nigeria, Ghana and Uganda since the system was established, first ostensibly for stabilization, and subsequently openly for taxation (at times euphemistically termed compulsory saving).

The imposition of most of these controls preceded the ascendancy of the current ideology. It was also quite unrelated to attempts to raise general living standards; its effect was the reverse, though it often benefited particular sectional interests. But for obvious reasons the system suits very well the exponents of the current ideology, which advocates close control of the economy. Moreover, the system also restricts economic contacts between these territories and the outside world and subjects these contacts to close government manipulation. These policies have created the framework of ready-made totalitarian states for the incoming governments. The various Western aid programs under British, American and United Nations auspices now play a large part in enabling and encouraging the African governments in this direction. They supply the finance and the personnel to help in the administering of such states, without which the African governments could not maintain closely controlled economies. With irrelevant exceptions (largely of a theoretical nature), foreign aid necessarily increases the hold of the governments over the economy, since it increases the resources of the government relative to the private sector. This is reinforced further when, as is now generally the case, preference in the allocation of aid is given to governments engaged in development planning.

These policies have also retarded or prevented the emergence of African groups of entrepreneurs and prosperous farmers who could be expected to resist extremist movements. They have enhanced the sense of dependence of the population both on the government and on the privileged industrial and commercial enterprises. And above all, they have greatly increased the prizes of political power and the intensity of the struggle for them. It is often said that the Europeans in Africa are afraid of the African majority. This is misleading. They are not afraid of the Africans. But in common with all other minorities, including African groups outside the government parties, they are reluctant to accept political domination by unlimited governments which closely and intensively control much of social and economic life. They well know that political independence has nothing to do with personal freedom.

X

Africa is huge and heterogeneous. Its economies do, however, exhibit certain common features which justify limited generalizations for certain purposes. For instance, they are generally poor. Again, subsistence production is comparatively important in most of them. Nevertheless, in the framing of policy their diversity must always be remembered. Policy recommendations, besides being based at least partly on value judgments, must also consider political and administrative possibilities. For this reason, policy proposals applicable to Africa as a whole would either have to be so vague and general as to be uninteresting, or if they were more specific they would fail to take account of the diversity of Africa. But I shall conclude with certain bald remarks which are relevant to development policy throughout Africa, even though they do not amount to generalized policy recommendations.

First, there is a wide range of essential tasks, in underdeveloped countries as elsewhere, which necessarily devolve on the government. These include: the management of foreign affairs to the best advantage of the country; the promotion of a suitable institutional framework for the activity of individuals; the maintenance of law and order; the control of the supply of money; the provision of basic health and education services, transport facilities, and of agricultural extension work. These are of the greatest importance in Africa, as elsewhere in the underdeveloped world. The establishment, shaping and adjustment of the institutional framework is a task of particular urgency, difficulty and complexity in rapidly changing conditions, especially in the transition from a subsistence to an exchange economy. The adequate performance of these tasks would exceed the slender resources of the governments of most or even all African countries, even in the absence of such ambitious tasks as comprehensive development planning. In many parts of Africa, as elsewhere in the underdeveloped world, the intense preoccupation with comprehensive planning has led to a neglect of the essential governmental tasks, and at the same time has obscured this neglect. It is paradoxical that the governments are engaged in extensive and close control over economic life when they cannot perform their essential functions.

Second, development, as a desirable aim of policy, cannot refer simply to the growth of output of physical commodities unrelated to the standard of living of the population.

Third, the axiomatic assumption which has come to be widely accepted that comprehensive development planning is an indispensable condition of economic progress is plainly unwarranted, since many countries in Africa, as elsewhere in both developed and underdeveloped areas, have progressed without it. Moreover, the suggestion does not show why or how government determination of the composition and direction of economic activity accelerates material progress, since this does not increase the volume of available resources but only centralizes their direction. Specific reasons rather than unsupported axiomatic assumptions need to be advanced why comprehensive development planning is likely to accelerate material progress. And it is clearly not a necessary general condition for economic development.

Fourth, the rapid development of many underdeveloped countries shows that the forces which promoted progress in the early history of the developed countries are often present in underdeveloped countries, unless obstructed by especially unfavorable human qualities and attitudes, social arrangements or political measures, or by lack of natural resources. Poverty or a late start in economic progress do not by themselves negate the relevance or potentialities of market forces.

Fifth, in Africa a large proportion of the people are subsistence producers. Subsistence production is incompatible with more than a very low standard of living. For rational framing of economic policy, it is essential to consider the effects of different measures on the ability or readiness of producers to progress from subsistence production to production for sale. This is relevant, for instance, to measures affecting the supply of consumer goods, to the level and incidence both of taxation and government expenditure, and to the regulation of land tenure.

Sixth, because of the poverty of Africa and the widespread presence of customs inimical to economic advance, the widening of contacts with the external world is particularly likely to be a condition of reasonably rapid economic progress. Measures designed to restrict these are almost certain to impede economic advance. The same applies to the severe restrictions on the immigration or activities of foreigners, whatever their merits on political grounds.

My last point concerns the granting and allocation of foreign aid. Government-to-government aid necessarily affects the political situation in the recipient country, since it increases the resources of the government relative to the private sector. There is no escaping from the involvement in the domestic situation. There seems to be good reason to suggest that if aid continues, it should be given to those governments which address themselves to the essential functions of government, the adequate discharge of which would strain their resources. There is an obvious value judgment in this point, but its relevance and basis are clear, particularly when it is remembered that devel-

opment, if it is to be meaningful, must refer to the progress of the standard of living of the population and not
simply to such partial or irrelevant indices as the output
of a particular sector, or the growth of a particular activity,
or even the volume of government expenditure.

Much of my argument goes counter to widely held notions. The reasoning may of course be wrong; but this has
to be established on criteria other than its popularity,
notably logical consistency or conformity with empirical
evidence. The validity of an argument does not depend
either on its popularity or on its political effectiveness. If
it did, then the National Socialist biological theories or the
labor theory of value would be scientifically valid.

4 Disengagement in Africa

ELSPETH HUXLEY

ELSPETH HUXLEY *was born in 1907 and brought up in Kenya where her parents were settlers. In 1931 she married Gervas Huxley, first cousin of Aldous and Julian Huxley; she accompanied him on extensive travels in various parts of the world and wrote books, travel articles and radio programs. During the war she worked in the BBC and the Colonial Office. After the birth of her son in 1944 she lived mainly on her farm in Wiltshire, England, as she does today. She served as a member of the Monckton Commission on the Federation of Rhodesia and Nyasaland in 1959–60. She has frequently been back to Kenya and to other parts of Africa.*

Beginning with a two-volume life of Kenya's pioneer, entitled White Man's Country: Lord Delamere and the Making of Kenya, *she has written over twenty books, including novels, travel books, and two autobiographical books. Her novel,* Red Strangers, *is about the Kikuyu tribe, and* The Walled City *is about Nigeria;* Four Guineas *is a travel book about West Africa, and* The Sorcerer's Apprentice *is about East Africa. Best known to American readers are her autobiographical books,* The Flame Trees of Thika *and* On the Edge of the Rift, *and her recent travel book,* With Forks and Hope, An African Notebook. *Her next novel will be entitled* A Man from Nowhere.

Mrs. Huxley is also a contributor to many publications,

including the British Sunday Times, Daily Telegraph, *and*
Punch, *and in America* Foreign Affairs, National Review,
and other periodicals.

The Myth of Freedom Fighters

All new nations need a set of myths to bolster up their
self-esteem. One aspect of the many-sided truth is picked
out and, like the speck of grit within the oyster, wrapped
in layers of legend and invention until the pearl is born:
compact, shining and romantic, the pearl of national pride.
Several generations later, it becomes the task of historians
to cut through these mythical accretions to examine the
grit of truth at the core—by then a hopeless task, but one
that gives employment to students and food for those arguments about themselves which so gratify the narcissistic
impulses of human beings.

True to this tradition, the newly independent states of
Africa are hard at work at myth-making. Their myth is
perhaps the oldest and simplest of all, that of the slave who
bursts his bonds and claims his freedom. The struggle
against colonialism, throwing off the yoke of the oppressor,
heroes whose blood was freely given for the cause—the
myth is growing at a speed proper to the tropics, and already warms the blood of young Africans.

The speck of grit at the heart of this oyster was that element of resistance offered by the colonial powers to African demands for political freedom. This has varied widely
both in its ideological basis, and in its practical expression.
At one extreme lay, and lies, the South African conviction
of the right, both divine and secular, of the white races to
maintain perpetual domination over black ones; at the
other the British intention, inherited from Indian days,
to fit her colonial peoples for self-rule and then withdraw

herself by stages, and hand over to an indigenous elite, duly trained and impregnated with the British ruling-class virtues of integrity, impartiality, moderation and administrative skill.

The policies of the French, Belgians and Portuguese have occupied, in general, a median position. The Portuguese have based their policy, as they still do, upon the theory that their colonies are integral parts of Portugal, constituent provinces as much provinces as Coruna or the Algarve, and incapable of detachment from the parent nation. From this it follows that African *assimilados* can become full Portuguese citizens, with all the rights and racial equality this entails, but cannot break away to run their own independent nations.

French Colonial Policy

A similar fiction inspired the French colonial theory of assimilation which they practiced in North and West Africa for a full century after the annexation of Algeria in 1842. Those Africans who qualified for French citizenship —always a small minority, as in the Portuguese territories— enjoyed full equality with Frenchmen and sent their deputies to the Assembly and the Senate in Paris. *Evolués* were admitted on equal terms into the civil service and professions and, by and large, encountered little of the color bar that so bruised feelings and sometimes embittered minds in other lands.

In time, the mythical foundation of these principles overcomes a natural human reluctance to admit the falsity of cherished dreams. The mirage of assimilation and the unity of *la France d'Outre-mer* gave way to a more realistic policy of "association," closer to the British standpoint. The French still tried to hold together their African territories in an association with the metropolitan country which was revamped in 1946 and called the *Union Fran-çaise*. This was short-lived. In 1956, under the inspiration of General de Gaulle, came the *loi cadre*, which marked France's acceptance of the postwar reality of African nationalism. No longer were France and her overseas territories to be politically united; autonomy for each of the separate entities was admitted as the goal. France had accepted "decolonization" in place of the assimilationist principle that had dominated her thinking for a hundred years.

But the end of political control did not, in French eyes, signify the end of French cultural influence or economic association—quite the reverse. By surrendering the one, she hoped to strengthen the others. General de Gaulle came up with the idea of French Community, to which all the major African leaders except those who had been lured into the Marxist parlor gave support; and in the referendum held in 1958 all the territories but Communist-led Guinea voted *"oui"* to the proposal that France's colonies should gain their full autonomy but remain in association both with each other, in a loosely federal setup, and with their former colonialist masters. Guinea went its own way.

The *loi cadre* came too late. The forces of a more extreme, chauvinistic form of nationalism were by then spreading over Africa like a bush fire. The Algerian war was probably the determining factor. In 1960, two years after its birth, the French Community in West and Equatorial Africa dissolved into a clutch of fourteen independent states, each with its vote in the United Nations. With the ex-ruling power, strong cultural and economic links remained and have been strengthened since 1960, but the political association disappeared.

Since 1960, the fourteen territories have grouped and regrouped like dancers taking part in the figures of some elaborate *pavanne*. Some have striven, and continue to strive, after a close federation with their neighbors. Some are drawn towards the so-called Casablanca nexus of interest in association with Nasser's Afro-Asian bloc; some towards the Guinea/Ghana axis with its revolutionary, quasi-Communist outlook, polarized by Nkrumah's powerful personality—*"l'agent provocateur des émotions de millions d'indigènes"* as he has been described; [1] but a majority towards the Brazzaville alliance in the *Union Africaine et Malgache* led by that dominant personality in French African politics, M. Félix Houphouët-Boigny, with its close links with France and its relatively stable and conservative outlook.

The speed and peacefulness with which France has liberated her former colonies is a remarkable phenomenon, taken too much for granted, perhaps, by the rest of the world. No less remarkable has been the mutual goodwill which has, on the whole, replaced the colonial association, and the degree of support France continues to give her ex-colonies. With each of them, save Guinea, she has defense agreements, and all are subsidized financially to an extent which makes the comparable British effort look derisory. It also evokes among French-speaking Africans an uneasy feeling that "neo-colonialism," in the shape of economic rather than political dependence, has sneaked in through the window while colonialism proper, in its political garb, has marched out of the door.

The Belgian Disaster

By contrast Belgian policy collapsed in a disaster which embroiled the world in one of its trickiest situations since the Suez crisis of 1956, and strained almost to breaking point the structure and prestige of the United Nations.

Typical, perhaps, of the outlook of the metropolitan

[1] Richard Wright, *Puissance Moiré*, Paris, 1955.

power, Belgian policy was, in its inspiration, economic through and through. While the French thought of spreading their culture and of their civilizing mission, and the British of their brand of parliamentary democracy, their law and their beliefs in tolerance, expedience, gradualism and seeing how things worked, the Belgians thought mainly in terms of development, trade, standards of living and the implanting of technical skills.

Their policy was not illiberal. In training Africans to perform technical and expert tasks they were, on the whole, in the van. They observed no economic color bar. They planned and spent to develop such desirable things as housing, medical services and industries. The United Nations' Trusteeship Council and its Visiting Missions found relatively little to criticize in their administration of the Trust Terrtory of (as it then was) Ruanda-Urundi.

The nub of Belgian colonial thinking was that economic progress should precede political development. They therefore suppressed political movements and parties and did nothing to train the Congolese to manage institutions of democracy. They would countenance no Congolese students in Belgian universities, other than prentice priests and doctors. Their endeavor was to isolate the Congolese politically from the rest of the world.

Whether or no this policy could have succeeded, given another fifty years, no one will ever know. It may be that it fell between two stools. Africans were neither encouraged to become black Belgians, nor to preserve and then develop their own native institutions through such means as indirect rule. Belgian rule was firm and somewhat rigid. But the Belgian Congo was not, in general, an unhappy country, nor a discontented one, before the debacle which followed the withdrawal of Belgian rule.

Why, then, did it happen? Primarily because the Belgians, having done nothing whatever to prepare the Congolese for self-rule, performed a sudden *volte-face* and decided to withdraw within two years. This was far too short a time to create even the flimsiest of administrations to take over. In this great, sprawling, undeveloped, unintegrated country, they left a vacuum. Not only that, but when the *Force Publique* mutinied—one of those accidents of history that can sometimes determine the course of events—some of the Belgians, their morale understandably low, lost their heads. The mutineers swept through the country, or those parts of it that mattered at the time, with murder, looting and rape. Panic spread, Belgians fled the country, law and order collapsed and that chaos came which so deeply embroiled the United Nations and led almost to the breakdown of its functions, to the death of Dag Hammarskjöld and to many other unfortunate and tragic events.

In spite of this, the remarkable thing is not that chaos came to the Congo when the Belgians pulled out, but that out of between thirty and forty states which have, in the last five or six years, emerged from their colonial status into full nationhood, only two have come to birth in open violence. (The other is the former Trust Territory of the Cameroons. Guinea nearly did, but not quite.) In all the rest, the passage has been smooth, the relations between the departing colonialists and their successors warm, friendly and based on mutual esteem.

The British Disengagement

Unlike the French, Belgians and Portuguese the British, true to their nature, had no rigid—or indeed, even nonrigid—theory of the place of colonies in the life of the nation. Britain has never based her actions on theories about anything; expediency and empiricism have determined her erratic course. Her merchants went abroad to trade and, where instability and disorder stultified their efforts, they sometimes managed to persuade a reluctant government to take steps, mainly through treaties of friendship with native potentates, which so embroiled them that withdrawal proved impossible, and before anyone really knew what had happened, a *de facto* British Protectorate had come into being.

The intention ultimately to withdraw from these imperial commitments—disengagement—has been implicit from the earliest days. Edmund Burke, debating Fox's East India Bill of 1783, may have been the first to express, in so many words, the idea of the trusteeship of advanced nations towards underdeveloped ones (as they came to be known), which found its latest embodiment in the Trusteeship Council of the United Nations.

Such rights or privileges [he observed, referring to political powers over the weak by the strong] are all, in the strictest sense, a trust; and it is of the very essence of every trust to be rendered accountable, and even totally to cease, when it substantially varies from the purpose for which it alone could have a lawful existence.[2]

Trusts are not wound up until the ward is of age and presumed to be capable of looking after his own affairs. That is the other half of the trusteeship principle: to fit the ward for his inheritance. In the colonial sphere, the outgoing power must train the dependent people for self-rule.

This British policy has always envisaged. One of the earliest statements was delivered by Lord Grey, then Secretary of State for the Colonies, during the administration of Lord John Russell in 1846–52. Britain's aim, he said, in West Africa was:

to train the inhabitants . . . in the arts of civilisation and

[2] Richard Corbett, *The Parliamentary History of England*, Vol. 22.

government, until they shall grow into a nation capable of pro-
tecting themselves and of managing their own affairs so that
the interference and assistance of the British authorities may
by degrees be less and less required.

That decolonization, as it is now called, and the transfer
of power back to the indigenous peoples were the objects
of British policy from the very start could not have been
more explicitly stated than it was in 1865, in a report ad-
vising on the future of the West African commitments into
which the Government was finding itself reluctantly
drawn, largely as a result of its efforts to suppress the
slave trade in what is now Nigeria. This Parliamentary
committee recommended:

That all further extension of territory or assumption of
Government, or new treaties offering any protection to native
tribes, would be inexpedient, and that the object of our policy
should be to encourage the natives in the exercise of those
qualities which may render it possible for us more and more to
transfer to them the administration of all the Governments,
with a view to our ultimate withdrawal from all, except, probably, Sierra Leone. [Sierra Leone was a special case because of
the settlements established at Freetown for freed slaves.] [3]

Much later, but no less clearly, a subsequent (and no
less aristocratic) Colonial Secretary propounded, in a famous statement of policy, the so-called Devonshire white
paper of 1923, the parallel doctrine that goes hand in hand
with that of withdrawal—the paramountcy of the interests
of the native peoples, over and above those of the subjects
of the colonial power.

His Majesty's Government think it necessary definitely to
record their considered opinion that the interests of the African natives must be paramount, and that if, and when, those

[3] Report of the Select Committee on Africa (Western Coast) 412, 1865.
Page XIV.

interests and the interests of the immigrant races should conflict, the former should prevail. . . . H.M.G. regard themselves
as exercising a trust on behalf of the African population.

This statement was made about Kenya, where, unlike any part of West Africa, white settlers had been encouraged to take up land and form a British community.
Even here, the twin objectives of withdrawal and African
self-rule were foreseen forty years ago. British colonial policy may not have been rigid, certainly at times it has been
muddled and contradictory, but, broadly speaking, it has
followed consistently a course towards disengagement plus
self-rule.

What, then, has all the fuss been about? How has anyone managed to create a legend of freedom fighters struggling to throw off the colonial yoke, when the owners of
that yoke were anxious to discard it? Where is the grit of
truth within the pearl of legend? For such a pearl has, in
fact, been created. There have been riots—small and un-
important ones, it is true, but still riots—in British dependencies; "prison graduates" with their caps of honor;
the banning of subversive movements; the bandying of
heated slogans; even Mau Mau. Africans have got their
legend, even if it is something of a milk and water one;
and no doubt it will grow.

The fuss has simply been about timing. A "gradual"
withdrawal was always foreseen. The white mentors would
not go until the black pupils had learnt their lessons thoroughly. These lessons included honest and competent administration, a democratic form of government, economic
viability, incorrupt justice and, especially in later years, at
least a skeleton of the basic welfare services such as health
and education.

What does "gradual" mean? How soon can people be
said to be "fit" for self-rule? Who is to decide these ques-

tions of timing and fitness—the outgoing colonialists, or the Africans themselves? It was these matters which divided trustee and ward, which caused the riots and prison graduates and, where there was a land problem as in Kenya, which underlay Mau Mau.

Once the Africans realized that the British meant to go, they echoed Macbeth: "If it were done when 'tis done, then 'twere well it were done quickly." The British played for time; not merely because to cling to power is a universal human inclination, but also from a genuine conviction that to hand over power to people who would abuse it, and without a cadre of trained and equipped indigenous leaders ready to replace the departing colonialists (as there was, for instance, in India when the British left in 1947) would be to betray the trust, not to implement it. So the conflict arose.

After some initial resistance, the British gave way, as they were bound to do. To fight for a principle can be justified; to fight for a little extra time cannot be a game worth the candle. The British did, in fact, do just that in Cyprus, and emerged deeply disillusioned and anxious to be rid as quickly as possible of any country bent on leaving the imperial nest. Algeria and Cyprus have been lessons in how *not* to decolonize which deeply impressed themselves on British public opinion.

Indirect Rule in British Dependencies

Between the wars, British colonial policy revolved round the system known as "indirect rule." This was to fit native peoples for their ultimate self-rule by recognizing and developing their own indigenous systems of government. Such systems varied from country to country but, in general, revolved in their turn round a hereditary ruler and his council of elders who, by long tradition, controlled the affairs of the tribe, or group of tribes making up a confederacy or kingdom. These political units ranged from a loose association of family patriarchs or village head-men, on the one hand, to, on the other, the Emirates of Nigeria, whose dignified and turbaned Muslim potentates held tight and effective sway over two or three million subjects. In every case the essence of the matter was that authority should be rooted in the traditions of the people and exercised at grassroot level by their own chiefs and leaders and not directly by the white official who, while his powers were wide and his activities many, was supposed to act as a guide, philosopher and friend, working behind the scenes, rather than as a giver of orders from ruler to subject.

It was also part of his task to "modernize" the indig-enous institutions which the British recognized, and en-shrined in legislation, in her dependencies. By this was meant the gradual—there is always this emphasis on grad-ualness in British policy—replacement of the hereditary system of installing rulers, by the elective principle. Na-tive authorities were to be "democratized"; the Emirs and Kabaka, the chief and king (deriving his authority, as often as not, from some divine or spiritual source) was eventually to be replaced by an elected district council, in itself to form a unit of a Western system of democracy based on British institutions. The point was that the tree of African government was not to be chopped down and replaced by an exotic seedling; rather was a democratic bud to be grafted on to the old stock of African tribalism.

Indirect rule was a principle taken over, like the ulti-mate aim of colonial policy, from India, where from the earliest days the authority of the Princes had been recog-nized. It was a cheap system, and relatively easy, at least in regions like Northern Nigeria, Ashanti and Buganda, where strongly centralized governments existed.

There were, of course, snags. One was that the native ruler, if sufficiently powerful, might come to resent British tutelage and work against, rather than with, the alien authority. Another was that in places it conflicted with the civilizing mission on which all colonial powers believed themselves to be embarked. Over and above the obligation to respect and develop traditional forms of government stood the obligation to introduce and spread Western, and Christian, principles of morality. Such practices as human sacrifice, cannibalism and slavery, native to pre-colonial Africa, had to be suppressed. Colonialists retained in their own hands the power to remove bad rulers and to be the judge of "good" and "bad" by Western standards.

In its heyday, indirect rule was regarded as the last word in enlightened colonial policy which, allied to the development of education, health and other welfare services, would transform the old, savage and barbaric Africa (as Europeans saw it) into a land of progressive, democratic, self-reliant citizens fully *au fait* with the practices of local government, modern taxation, the committee system and parliamentary debate, without the sacrifice of their own institutions and customs of a non-repugnant kind. Evolution, not revolution, was the British aim. Sir Donald Cameron, one of its foremost exponents (trained under the great Sir Frederick, later Lord, Lugard in Nigeria, he introduced the system into Tanganyika) summed it up in the words:

. . . it is our duty to do everything in our power to develop the native on lines which will not Westernise him and turn him into a bad imitation of a European. . . . We want to make him a good African.

This was the antithesis of the French assimilation policy, whose aim was to turn the African into a good imitation Frenchman.

Nationalist leaders who emerged since 1948, however,
were disenchanted. They attacked indirect rule on the
grounds that it perpetuated tribalism. Twenty years ago,
even perhaps ten, this would have been no crime. Tribalism was, and still is, a fact, one of the basic facts of African
life. Africans were proud of their tribe, just as Europeans
are proud of their nation and Americans, in addition, of
their state. Only recently has tribalism become a dirty
word.

The reason is that it divides Africans instead of uniting
them, and then weakens and confuses them. It looks back
toward a past which they now wish to sweep under the car-
pet, rather than forward towards a puissant and united set
of nations, or even a Pan-African federation that, after
centuries of insignificance and being pushed around, in-
tends at long last to make its voice heard in the world and
to push around other nations. Tribalism has become a
symbol of the old, enslaved, despised Africa, to be overcome as quickly and completely as possible by education,
national unity and "African socialism." So indirect rule
was one of the first nationalist targets of attack and it was
shot down, well and truly, before the British withdrawal,
to be replaced by a system of elected councils based on universal suffrage and controlled by the political party that in
turn controls the state. In Tanganyika, for instance, where
indirect rule almost became a British fetish, the "Native
Authorities" through which the country was governed
were abolished by the ruling party, the Tanganyika African National Union, before the British withdrawal. The
office of chief has been abolished and the chiefs themselves either discredited or, if sufficiently educated and
locally respected, taken on as salaried servants of the local

authority. All those so employed must be members of, and loyal to, TANU, which has a total and unchallenged control of the whole of Tanganyika's government, central and local. For this former Trusteeship territory of the United Nations has emerged as a classic example of the uninhibited single-party state, dedicated to a speedy realization of "African socialism."

Tanganyika and the United Nations

How has this come about? Has the influence of the Trusteeship Council of the United Nations, under whose aegis Tanganyika developed between 1946 and 1961, led, however inadvertently, to the triumph of the single-party state, even before independence? Or would this have happened anyway? What, in fact, has the influence of the United Nations amounted to?

There is, of course, no clear-cut answer to these questions. The only measure of the influence of the United Nations would seem to lie in the difference between the course of events in Tanganyika and in those African dependencies ruled without reference to the United Nations by the Administering Authority, in this case Britain. (The same would apply, *pari passu*, to the other Trusteeship Territories administered by France and Belgium.) The short answer in this case is that there is no obvious difference; all the other African countries directly administered by Britain have attained, or very shortly will attain, their independence; Tanganyika was not even the first, but followed the Sudan, Ghana and Nigeria. The inference therefore is that the trusteeship of the United Nations had no significant effect upon Tanganyika's political development.

To some extent, this is borne out by a careful study of the question published in 1961 by Dr. B. G. T. Chidzero

under the title *Tanganyika and International Trusteeship.*
Although, he concluded, British colonial policy has often
been swayed, and sometimes deflected, by expediency, "the
principles and objectives characteristic of international
trusteeship correspond closely to the best principles and
objectives in British policy." There has been no conflict in
aim.

But this is not to say that the Trusteeship Council has
exercised *no* influence—or only that, as Professor Schwar-
zenberger observed in *Power Politics,* of a "nuisance
value." The nuisance value has certainly been there, especially in connection with the right of any citizen of a
Trusteeship Territory to present a petition to the General Assembly. Some pretty flimsy grievances have been
aired. And the opportunities offered to member states of
the United Nations hostile to the Western European powers to use the Assembly and the Council as platforms for
attack in their political war on the West have been too
strong, obvious and numerous to be resisted. The anti-
Western nations have made the most of them. Nevertheless, Dr. Chidzero concludes, there *has* been a United
Nations influence, and it has been far from negligible. In
brief, it has been to act as a spur.

While, in general, "there are no radical differences between the position and the attitude of the British on the
one hand and that of the United Nations on the other,"
the differences which have been evident have concerned
the speed of development. Gradualism has been the British intention—gradual, vegetable growth to allow changes
to sink in and become assimilated, to allow time for trial
and error, above all (as we have seen) to allow time for
the training of Africans not only in the skills and crafts
of administration and management, but in practical experience.

"There is much virtue," said Sir Andrew Cohen, "in proceeding step by step, neither too quickly nor too slowly, judging the exact nature of each step in the light of experience of the last one, and consulting the representatives of the people at each stage."

The Trusteeship Council has been against gradualism. From about 1954 onwards, its members pressed continuously for the setting up of target dates for the achievement of independence. In this, as in other respects, they backed the African nationalists as against the Administering Authority; they were continuously urging the man at the wheel to take his foot off the brake.

"By its attitude," Dr. Chidzero sums up, "the Trusteeship Council has thrown its tremendous weight behind the Africans' cause. . . . This is probably the most important influence of the Council on political developments in the territory." Its influence has "had the effect of keeping the political life of the Territory in a constant state of flux."

A Question of Franchise

In at least one respect the United Nations has influenced the direction, as distinct from the speed, of events. This has lain in their insistence on universal suffrage as the immediate goal, rather than the qualified franchise which was favored by the Administering Authority.

On the face of it, this might seem a technicality; but it has in fact been the decisive factor in the modern history of Tanganyika—and, indirectly, of Kenya as well. It decided that the nature of change should be revolutionary, not evolutionary. It killed stone-dead the policy of multi-racialism whereby Britain had hoped to protect the interests of minority groups settled in East Africa, achieve a steady economic growth, and curb the excesses of African nationalism.

In East Africa, unlike the West African countries which

led the way into independence, so-called "immigrant communities" of non-African races have lived as settlers, not as birds of passage, in the case of Asians for about a thousand years, in the case of Europeans for about sixty. Most of the Asians came of their own accord to trade; Europeans came as traders, missionaries and experts, but also as farmers, settling permanently (as they believed) on the land; and many of them came as a direct result of Government encouragement.

In Tanganyika, this policy of encouraging European settlers to take up undeveloped land in the interior, mainly in order to raise produce to be carried out by railroads built for strategic and humanitarian reasons, was started by the Germans before World War I, and in Kenya by the British about the same time. Inevitably, the introduction of the settler element gave a twist to policy unknown in non-settler countries, where the path to African self-rule was unimpeded by the interests of other communities.

That "white settlement" has been directly encouraged and initiated by Governments is of cardinal importance. As a result, the governments concerned had, and were conscious of, obligations towards the settlers. They had made certain promises—public, repeated and specific promises— to protect the interests, political as well as economic, of the settlers they had invited in, and as time went on it became clear as daylight that these promises conflicted with the equally clear obligations accepted by the British Government towards the Africans who looked to a speedy achievement of self-rule. So discrepant were the numbers—blacks in Tanganyika outnumbered whites by about 400 to one, in Kenya by about 200 to one—that African self-rule on a basis of one-man-one-vote inevitably meant the political extinction of the Europeans. Once more playing for time, the British hoped to bridge the enormous gap between the interests, claims and, to some extent, legitimate expectations of the two communities (or three, with the Asians —but society breaks down into "immigrant" and "indigenous" communities) by a policy that became known by the clumsy name of multiracialism.

The Multiracial Policy

Multiracialism meant that for political purposes minority groups would be treated as communities, rather than as a collection of individuals. On the Legislative Councils, Europeans, Asians and Africans were allotted so many seats for each community. At first the whites commanded a majority; gradually African numbers were increased with the aim of preponderance; but even when this was achieved, small but still significant blocs or parties representing the immigrant races, and elected by race, were to survive.

This policy recognized racialism as a fact, just as indirect rule recognized tribalism, and built upon it a political system. It was never envisaged as more than a stopgap policy. But a stopgap can perform a useful, indeed an indispensable, service. If you don't stop gaps, floods pour through them. This is what happened. The stopgap policy became anathema to African nationalists, and was demolished in the name of democracy.

The political core of the policy of multiracialism was the qualified franchise. Certain qualifications were needed before a citizen's name could be accepted on a voters' register. These as a rule were simple and basic, involving merely age, a limited degree of literacy, and sometimes an additional qualification of property or status. (Chiefs, headmen, soldiers and parsons, for instance, would qualify, even if they couldn't read or write.)

A basic intention of the qualified franchise was ultimately to do away with racialism by submitting everyone, of any race, to the same tests. In fact, of course, the imposition of any kind of test admitted, for the time being, virtually all the Europeans and only a small minority of relatively educated Africans. That was the intention—to slow things down. It was a practical expression of the old adage propounded by Cecil Rhodes—"equal rights for all civilized men."

Satisfactorily to define the word "civilized" has always been impossible. This was merely an attempt to take the political measure of the term, and it boiled down to literacy plus some small stake in the country's economy, either through property or services rendered. The multi-racial policy was, as Dr. Chidzero sums it up, "a device for delaying the advent of rule by the African majority. Through it, the British hoped to gain time for a transition period during which the racial groups would learn to sink their differences and achieve voluntary interracial, or supraracial, cooperation." Its first official recognition was perhaps a statement in the House of Commons made in 1952 by Mr. Oliver Lyttleton, then Secretary of State for the Colonies. The British Conservative Government, he said, interpreted the trusteeship agreement, in the case of Tanganyika, as an obligation

to provide for the full participation of all sections of the population, irrespective of race or origin, in the progressive development of political institutions and in the economic and social advancement of the territory. Each section of the population must be enabled to play its full part in the development of the territory and its institutions in complete confidence that the rights and interests of all communities, both indigenous and immigrant, will be secured and preserved.

If ever there was an attempt to have your cake and eat it, this was it. The policy was bound to fail, and it did. The tragedy was that so many Europeans and Asians, naturally anxious to believe that a Government which had so often stressed the value of their services in building the economic structure of the countries concerned would not abandon them to a flood of African nationalism, believed what they were so portentously told. In fact, of course, the Government was promising what it could not perform, and this, no doubt, they should have recognized.

Partnership

In Kenya and Tanganyika, the multiracial policy held up for about seven or eight years and then collapsed. In Central Africa it has lasted longer. Reinforced by the weight of a strongly entrenched white settler and mining community under the taurine leadership of Sir Roy Welensky, it became the foundation of the Federation of Rhodesia and Nyasaland launched with high white hopes and deep black fears in 1953, and broken up, after many painful struggles, by the forces of African nationalism at Victoria Falls just ten years later.

Here in Central Africa it was known as the policy of partnership and adopted as a guiding light by Sir Roy Welensky's United Federal Party, which ruled the Federation for its brief spell, if not of glory, then of economic development and political unease. That that partnership was a front behind which white commercial and political interests had their way, with no genuine attempt to bring the African races into full partnership, was an accusation widely leveled at the federalists. In this there was some truth; but, however genuine the partnership ideal had been, and whatever steps might have been taken to translate the ideal into practice, it is exceedingly unlikely that the African nationalists, headed by such personalities as Dr. Hastings Banda of Nyasaland and Mr. Kenneth Kuanda of Northern Rhodesia, would have for a moment contemplated settling for anything less than full adult suffrage and, therefore, the unrestricted dominance of the African majority.

The direction was decided, and nothing could have changed it. Multiracialism was a brake. It failed to hold back the vehicle by more, perhaps, than two or three years; and the full weight of the United Nations, whose Visiting Mission condemned the policy in 1954, and the Trusteeship Council, which consistently opposed it, was directed towards maneuvering the Administering Authority into taking its foot off the pedal. In East Africa, with all three countries independent on a basis of universal suffrage and with all-African Governments, the triumph of nationalism as against multiracialism is now complete; there is no protection (in white terminology) or privilege (the black equivalent) for minority groups, whose individuals must take their chance as citizens like any others, of whatever race, color or persuasion.

Multiracialism is no less dead in Nyasaland and in Northern Rhodesia, but in the third member state of the now defunct Federation, Southern Rhodesia, whose government is still controlled by the white minority, partnership and a qualified franchise remain the basis of policy. A population of some quarter of a million whites rules over some three million Africans. How long this can last is a guess no man would care to make—any more than he would, if he were wise, predict the future of the Republic of South Africa, with its three million whites committed to apartheid sitting on the heads of some ten million Africans.

The Time Factor

The tragedy of both the British and the French in Africa, still more of the Belgians, is that the time needed to fulfill their policies, which were sensible in design and reasonably well-intentioned, was not allowed. It is probably true that they did not pay enough attention to this factor of time. They assumed too easily that it stretched before them and need not be carefully measured; at one time they talked of generations before Africans could be educated and economically raised to a level where they would be "fit" to rule themselves. There was no sense of urgency.

When all that is said, it is also true that no one could have foreseen, or did foresee, the mounting speed with which events have raced onwards in the last decade. The colonial powers (so far with the exception of Portugal) have been hustled off the scene like cattle driven to the roundup. None of their policies has had a chance to mature. A measure of the unexpectedness of the speed is given by the fact that the United Nations Visiting Mission to Tanganyika in 1954 estimated that the country would be ready for self-rule in twenty to twenty-five years. This statement was derided by British administrators as being far too precipitate; some of the Africans themselves thought it unrealistic; even Mr. Julius Nyerere, then regarded as the fieriest and more impatient of nationalists, spoke of ten to twelve years. In fact, independence came in seven.

The role of the United Nations, as we have seen, has been that of spur, goad and accelerator; the Trusteeship Council has endeavored to keep things in "a state of flux." Whether this has rendered a service either to the Africans who are taking over these half-fledged, undeveloped territories, or to the world at large and to the cause of general peace remains to be seen. Goads are often needed; so, on occasion, are halters. It all depends on whether you are dealing with a lazy, fat old cob or with an angry young stallion. The United Nations has concentrated on the plodding Dobbin of colonialism, and tried to placate the angry stallion by gentle pats on its arched neck.

After the Nationalist Victories

Nationalism has now won its battle virtually without a fight all over Africa except, for the time being, in Southern Rhodesia, the Republic of South Africa, and in Angola and Mozambique. The struggle is won, the myths are in the process of creation and the question now is: what next?

Two trends have become plain. One is for the newly independent states to gang up, with a mounting ferocity and by fair means and foul, against these surviving colonialist powers in order to drive them from the continent, if necessary—and if practicable—by force. The other is to crack down with equal determination on internal elements of opposition to the present nationalist rulers, and to set up in perpetuity the single-party state.

Both these African resolves have bruised the illusions of those Western liberals who are willing to look facts in the face. That the new African nations would be lovers both of peace and of democracy was among the firmest of their beliefs. Western liberals taught Africans their brand of democracy and believed Africans already had a natural love of peace.

Why they should have entertained such notions is a mystery; certainly nothing could be further from the truth. Africans are probably no more and no less peace-loving than men of any other color, creed or race. That is to say, their history is one long record of warfare, bloodshed, conquest and strife, just like the record of other peoples, nations and races, from Siberia to Spain, from Prussia to Peru. The only difference is that hitherto Africans have proved less inventive than other peoples, whether in the arts of peace or the devices of war; they have managed with spears, arrows and assegais, where paler-skinned races have devised gunpowder, cannon, mortar, bazooka, flamethrower, bomber, nuclear warhead and Polaris submarine. This lack of ingenuity is not correlated with pacific intention, merely with a tendency to make do with things as they are, rather than endeavor constantly to improve them, and thereby to enjoy more leisure, rather than be obliged to toil without respite to keep pace with events and possess the newest toys.

African Democracy

As for democracy, the African claim is that Africans had their own version of it long before the Western nations tried to impose upon them that particular form favored by the colonizing power, whether the "Westminster model" or the constitution of whatever French Republic was currently extant. The African version was rooted in family and village, in tribe and council and the chief who, far from being (as a rule) a despot, was a mouthpiece for the decision of a hierarchy of councillors who in turn voiced the corporate intentions of the tribe.

Now that they are free, Africans wish to adapt their own forms of democratic government to modern conditions and to jettison colonialist, Western forms. This in practice (so runs the argument) boils down to the single-party state. This is not, in the view of such protagonists as Dr. Julius Nyerere, M. Houphouët-Boigny and M. Léopold Senghor, and even of Dr. Nkrumah and M. Sékou Touré (whose outlook is far closer to the authoritarian position than that of the first-named trio) a form of dictatorship. Opposition is there, it is voiced and not suppressed—but at a different stage. Criticism, opinion and complaint must be voiced within the party, the single party, at a branch level; conflicts must be sorted out before they rise to the top; at the top, there must be unity and unquestioned loyalty to the head of state.

Naturally this thesis has attracted a great deal of both dissension and support. Is it viable or specious? *Can* you have democracy without an organized opposition—without the possibility of changing the government by peaceful votes of the majority? Is not this the crux? Such questions can be argued, and have been and will be argued till the cows come home. For practical purposes, argument is beside the point. A one-party regime has been established within the last two or three years in almost every former colonial territory; in some cases, as in Ghana and in Tanganyika, it was entrenched even before the colonial power withdrew. Algeria, by the overwhelming vote of its citizens in a referendum, is the latest to decide in favor of single-party rule. The Sudan led the way by setting up a military dictatorship. The only notable exception is Nigeria, a federation of three powerful semi-autonomous Regions plus a small fourth slice carved off two of them, and, in each of these Regions, there is virtual single-party rule. The leaders of the Opposition in one of them, the Western Region, have recently been obliged to share the fate of most Opposition leaders, having been jailed for long periods after a verdict of "guilty" to charges of conspiring to overthrow the state.

Single-party rule in Africa, we may then take it, is a *fait accompli;* democracy as Western nations understand it has not survived the colonialists who introduced it by more than a few years. It is useless to bemoan this situation. The plain fact is that, however undesirable in theory, it was in practice inevitable. The reason is that there was no such thing, before independence, as an African nation. All were deeply divided along tribal and racial lines. All were abstractions on maps created by colonialists during the period of the so-called "scramble" and by means of adjustments made through the years.

The first need of all the newly independent governments is to create the countries over which they preside: to instill a national consciousness and sense of unity into the people. This can be done only through strong, determined and above all stable central control. Any other expedient could lead to only one result: the disintegration of the countries in a welter of internal rivalries for power, accompanied by intrigue, plotting and eventual civil war. To forestall chaos, Africa has thrown up its Nkrumahs and Tourés, its Bandas and Nyereres and Kenyattas and Abbouds, as the bloodstream of a healthy man throws up antibodies to destroy the bacilli that would otherwise destroy the man.

It is a truism that to create unity one needs a common foe. There must be an enemy at the gate in order to unite those within. That enemy is still colonialism, even though colonialism is a dead horse—a doomed one anyway, driven to its last corral south of the Zambesi, northeast of the Drakensberg and northwest of the Kalahari desert.

African Unity

In order to drive the vestiges of colonialism from their last entrenchments, black Africa must unite. This is the motive force behind the new and militant version of Pan-Africanism which, starting as a "back-to-Africa" movement, of a nature similar to Zionism, among Negro intellectuals in the United States and the West Indies, now aims at a political and military alliance between all the black African states.

Alliances can be defensive or aggressive. This modern version of Pan-Africanism (so very different from the old) could, in a sense, be said to be defensive against the neo-colonialism in which all African states see a threat to their true independence. It can also be, and is, exceedingly aggressive, and makes no bones about it, in regard to the Republic of South Africa and Portugal.

The speed and strength with which this militant spirit will grow is likely to depend, to some extent at least, on the outcome of a tussle for leadership now going on behind the scenes between dedicated nationalists with Marxist leanings ranged behind Presidents Nkrumah and Sékou Touré, and those whom Westerners consider, not without an element of wishful thinking, to be more moderate in outlook, such as Presidents Nyerere and Houphouët-Boigny and the Emperor Haile Selassie.

Hitherto Africans have lacked the means, the power and the resources to impose their wills and ideologies on other nations and peoples. They have been fully preoccupied in setting up their own establishments. This phase is coming to an end. Like other peoples flexing muscles newly developed, they have begun to feel the urge actively to influence the course of world affairs. After being pushed around themselves for centuries, they are understandably desirous of doing a little pushing around of other people. And the means, power and resources are all going their way. Western nations, largely as conscience-money, are providing the means and will increasingly do so through their programs to aid underdeveloped countries. The power they are groping for, not least through the Afro-Asian bloc in the United Nations. This power, largely that of numbers in terms of votes in the Assembly, of determination and a waxing confidence, they will surely use with growing skill and resolution. They are beginning to get the Western nations on the run, and know it; and they are not likely to hold back.

The resources they will assemble partly through the pooling process which lies behind the Pan-African movement, now crystallized in the Organization of African Unity set up in mid-1963 with headquarters in Addis

Ababa, with its defense pacts, and partly through playing off the enemies of Western nations in the Communist world. Few of their leaders are committed Marxists, but almost all share a general outlook vaguely known as "African socialism." This has never been precisely defined. The recent announcement by Mr. Ben Bella that the former French-owned Algerian estates of any size are to be nationalized, split up and redistributed among peasants, suggests that African socialism, if this is a sample, differs little, in practice, from any other kind.

Western students, politicians and commentators have made intermittent attempts over the last twenty years to assess the influence of the United Nations on African affairs. They still think in these terms. This is out of date. What will in future be needed is to assess the influence of the thirty-three independent African nations—a number which will soon rise to between thirty-five and forty—on the United Nations, and on the rest of the world.

That influence, already considerable, may soon grow as rapidly as the number of African states themselves has grown in the last five or six years. It is a forced growth, and the leaders are young and inexperienced. Africans are flushed with pride of victory and feel the world to be their oyster; they mean to prize it open with a sharp knife. Populations are increasing at a rate which cannot but terrify; their poverty is great and growing, means of employment lacking, they are bottled up inside their countries and yet are told they have inherited the earth. The situation is revolutionary.

CLOSE-UPS

5 A Black African Speaks

K. A. Busia

K. A. Busia *was born in 1913 in the Gold Coast (Ghana).*
After training at Wesley College at Kumasi and Achimota
College in his native land, he received a B.A., M.A., and
D.Phil. in Social Anthropology at Oxford University. Sub-
sequently, he served as a District Commissioner of the
Gold Coast from 1942 to 1949 and was in charge of the
Sociological Survey of the Gold Coast Government, 1947–
49. From 1949 to 1954 he was on the faculty of the Uni-
versity of the Gold Coast.

From 1951 to 1959, Dr. Busia was a member of the Legis-
lative Assembly of Ghana, and he became the Leader of the
Opposition in the Ghana Parliament from 1956 to 1959.
When this position was made untenable by Nkrumah,
Dr. Busia went into exile. He is presently Guest Professor
at St. Antony's College, Oxford.

His books include The Position of the Chief in the
Modern Political System of Ashanti *(1951) and* The Challenge of Africa *(1962); he has written several* West African
Affairs Pamphlets, *prepared papers for the Third World*
Congress of Sociology and the International African In-
stitute, contributed to several symposia, and appeared in
such periodicals as the Journal of World History, *the* International Social Science Bulletin, *the* Archives de Soci-
ologie des Religions, *and* The Atlantic Monthly.

The most striking fact about contemporary Africa is the emergence of independent nations from colonial rule. Since 1957, some thirty new African nations have been admitted to membership in the United Nations. This has not only strengthened the voice of Africa in that forum of nations but has also helped to focus world attention on its problems. These problems center around the demand for the ending of European domination in any part of the continent, the recognition of racial equality and the attainment of racial justice, and the general concern for speedy economic and social development.

The shout for freedom heard in recent years in different tongues all over Africa not only expresses the desire for independence but also gives the reason for the demand for ending foreign domination. A stage in history has been reached where all peoples of Africa want to be free to manage their own affairs, whether domestic or external. The countries that are already free are engaged with nation building. All the new nations begin within political boundaries created by colonial powers. Within this framework, they have their own internal problems of developing a sense of nationhood. They need to inculcate or stimulate that sense of belonging together which is an essential criterion of nationhood. Along with this they seek to raise living standards and also ensure their self-defense. Independence brings its inescapable responsibilities.

All the new nations of Africa realize and accept the responsibility for rapid economic development. They have all been characterized as "underdeveloped." Besides the low productivity which this characterization emphasizes, the countries of Africa have also been marked by poor communications, physical isolation, and a high degree of illiteracy. Most of the people who live in Africa have earned their living by farming, usually subsistence farming. The technological equipment has consisted of simple, comparatively inefficient tools, rather than machines. Until recently, African economies have been of very slow growth. Even where cash crops were introduced, there was little of the specialization which comes with industrialization. With little specialization and inefficient tools, output and standards of living are generally low, and economic growth is a basic requirement for social development. In the conditions prevailing in Africa, it has been frequently pointed out that public utilities like roads, harbors, railways and telecommunications are prerequisites of economic growth. Their lack or inadequacy makes it difficult to increase productivity rapidly. These deficiencies often accompany other human needs as well: poor health and high mortality rates due to the absence or paucity of health services; water-borne diseases from impure drinking water; and the lack of skills for industry. Thus schools, training centers, public-health measures, water supplies, housing and similar services have also to be listed among the prerequisites of economic growth.

These utilities have to be paid for, and since the agricultural communities of Africa have little to spare for savings and investment, the initial stage is always difficult. Outside aid is needed. The problem of economic development in Africa is made more difficult by the impact of the industrialized countries. Industrial products from these countries have flooded the markets in Africa and killed or threatened to kill indigenous crafts; foreigners from industrial countries have gone out to Africa to provide management or skilled labor, because there is no time to wait for the development of local skills. It is in the face of such conflicts that African countries must compete for economic growth. At the pace at which they feel compelled to go, they cannot provide the necessary capital or skilled manpower from their own resources.

Developments since the Second World War mark a new

stage in the economic development of Africa—the establishment of secondary industries to provide some of the goods formerly imported from abroad. These industries cover a varied list: materials for building, such as cement, nails and tiles, or for clothing, such as textiles and shoes; factories for making furniture; mills for processing oil, flour, sugar, coffee, rubber or tobacco; breweries; bakeries and factories for making biscuits and confectionery; and service and repair shops for bicycles, cars and radio sets. Development plans launched by various African countries show that there are schemes for large rubber and sugar plantations, mechanized state farms, large dams and hydroelectric power, and even heavy industry, based on iron, coal, bauxite or aluminum. Africa has entered a period of industrial revolution from subsistence economies to cash crop production and secondary and heavy industry.

Though the need for outside aid is recognized, for economic as well as for political reasons the new nations of Africa have to be cautious in receiving it. The needed equipment, personnel, skills, know-how or capital could come in on terms which might stifle their newly won independence. Hence, suspicions of "neo-colonialism." Some nationalists have extended neo-colonialism to cover an assortment of things: the American Peace Corps; the proposed East African Federation; defense agreements and bases, particularly when they are the subject of pacts with former colonial powers; or association with the Common Market of the Six. All this underscores the fear of exploitation. The new nations of Africa are prepared to accept aid, provided it ensures continued national independence and freedom. The national independence they wish to preserve cannot, it may be noted, mean self-sufficiency, or an economic stage where they will no longer need the industrial countries. This is worth stressing, for clearly we have reached a stage in scientific and technological development where it is unrealistic to consider independence in this way. What the new nations of Africa wish to preserve, primarily, is the right to make their own decisions rather than have them made for them. They do not want aid which will tie them to one or another of the blocs of the industrial countries. They do not want aid to be a factor in the unfortunate Cold War that divides East and West.

This is where the United Nations comes in. Many of the African states prefer aid through the United Nations or through multi-national arrangements. This, it is argued, prevents any country from exercising undue influence, or from using aid as a means of tying the beneficiaries in Africa to its own policy.

Unfortunately the problem is a complex one. Aid has both economic and political consequences. On the economic side, there is a relation between aid and trade, and this has implications for the countries in Africa as well as the industrial countries. Giving aid in terms of machinery or capital or personnel raises attendant issues. The countries in Africa will use this aid not only to improve their agriculture and increase its productivity, but also, as indicated by what is already being done, to industrialize. They will be able to buy more from the industrial countries, but they will also be in a position to sell more. The industrial countries should not only be prepared to give aid in order that the countries of Africa may produce more goods, but they should also be prepared to buy more from Africa. Some of the goods Africa will have to sell may include items that she buys at present from the industrial countries. It must be recognized that increasing aid to Africa must change the patterns of trade; but this can forge new links, a new interdependence rather than independence which is becoming increasingly anachronistic.

There are political aspects and implications too. Politics and economics are inextricably linked. It can be argued that substantial economic aid given to the government of a country ultimately underwrites the political policies of that government. I think it justifiable for any country to admit that the aid it is prepared to give to other countries is done out of self-interest, and not unadulterated altruism. Such a position is not necessarily wrong. All nations, for example, have, or should have, self-interest in helping one another; self-interest in narrowing the gap between the rich countries and the poor, because this would make for happy relations and ensure world peace; and all have a right to self-interest in the preservation of world peace. This, for example, was recognized by the Council of the North Atlantic Treaty Organization when, in its Declaration of Principles in December 1959, it expressed "interest in the maintenance of peace and the development of conditions of stability and political and economic well-being in the vitally important continent of Africa." Obviously, one nation could justifiably exercise a right to withhold aid from another, if it had reason to believe that such aid would help the other nation to pursue policies that would lead to war.

There are other political considerations connected with aid, such as those concerning ideologies. It is a moot point whether these should influence aid. The United Nations as a forum for all nations may not itself be in a position to consider aid in relation to political ideologies; but it cannot prevent the constituent members who provide the aid from doing so. There are examples to show that it would be unrealistic to regard ideological controversies as irrelevant to considerations of aid to African countries, even if all such aid were channeled through the United Nations.

It can be shown that attention has been given by some countries to political trends in Africa as factors relevant to economic aid. All the new states of Africa regard economic development to be a paramount need. There are policies

directed towards planning and central control of the use of
both human and material resources; in the context of
Africa this has included state enterprises in industry, finance and marketing. All this has tended to increase the
role of the state. In some of the new countries of Africa it
has led to a conscious effort to establish one-party regimes,
a number on avowedly Marxist-Leninist lines; in others,
aware of the dangers of one-party regimes for true freedom
and civil liberties, one-party regimes are strongly resisted.
It has been argued that the single party is more appropriate to the economic and social conditions of Africa; that,
in contrast with the disunity and factionalism and even
subversion which a multi-party system may encourage, the
single party allows for united effort and free discussion;
and also that the single party is in keeping with traditional
methods of reaching decisions on the basis of consensus.
But it can and should be asked whether one-party regimes
encourage the development of free institutions. Many
would agree that they do not. However, the United Nations must exist on the basis of tolerance of diversity, and
political trends in Africa should be considered from the
standpoint of a sympathetic understanding of the problems
of democracy and freedom in new nations. It cannot be
denied, nevertheless, that so far the framework of the one-
party regimes has been more like that used by dictators in
Europe than like the parliamentary systems of the democracies of the West. It may be argued that one-party regimes
in Africa do not necessarily spell dictatorships, and that
the single party can be an instrument for transforming
society by persuasion and agreement and without curtail-
ing civil liberties. But these arguments have not so far
been demonstrated as facts. A nation without an antece-
dent of parliamentary rule, handicapped by illiteracy and
poverty, with an ineffective, inarticulate, or unheeded
public opinion, and with a legacy of authoritarian, pater-

nalistic colonial rule, is extremely vulnerable to the encroachments of tyranny. Many African nations are in this situation, and some of their emergent one-party regimes have been accompanied by stringent and indiscriminately applied Preventive Detention Acts; the suppression of criticism and opposition; central control of mass media of communication, especially press and radio; increased security measures; and mass imprisonments, not only of those opposed to the ruling party, but also of members of the ruling party who venture to criticize. Ghana is the most conspicuous example.

Questions are therefore raised, not only as to whether one-party regimes provide the stability and freedom they claim to do, but also whether they do not in fact aid one side against the other in the ideological conflict between East and West. Though such an issue may be directly avoided when aid is given through the United Nations and its agencies, individual countries contributing to such aid may feel an obligation to consider the policies and values the aid helps to institute or perpetuate. As far back as 1947, Marshall, then Secretary of State of the United States, in a famous speech at Harvard on June 5, stated that United States policy "should be the revival of a working economy in the world so as to permit the emergence of political and social conditions in which *free institutions can exist.*" It would be consistent with this policy for the United States to deny aid which would help the stifling of free institutions. Indeed, there are instances when certain countries, such as France and Russia, have refused to pay contributions to United Nations operations, for example, in the Congo, because they disapproved of the policies. America has refused aid to Cuba, and more recently has withheld aid to Pakistan, on grounds which can be regarded as expressing disapproval of the policies of those countries. Should such considerations apply in the case of

aid to Africa? Whether one agrees with these specific decisions or not, the fundamental issue they raise is one of responsibility: whether a nation contributing economic aid
to another, whether through bilateral or multilateral arrangements or through the United Nations, has the right,
nay the responsibility, to make its decision on the basis of
the possible consequences of the results of the aid, as far as
it can judge them. I do not think that international aid, in
whatever form, should avoid moral and ethical considerations, even though this must mean that there will be dis-
agreements. The preservation of peace cannot mean the
abandonment of moral responsibility. International aid is
itself the acceptance of moral responsibility by the rich to
help the not-so-well-off.

There should, of course, be tolerance of diversity. This
implies the recognition of differences in mutual respect,
and it introduces another issue of vital concern to all African countries—race relations. Mutual respect must be
based on a recognition of racial equality. The new leaders
of Africa are united in pointing out that the fact that the
countries of Africa have lower standards of living does not
prove that Africans belong to inferior races. There is no
correlation between productivity and genetics; there is, in
fact, sometimes the suspicion that the aid which industrial
countries offer may be paternalistic expressions of their
racial superiority; hence, the desire that conditions should
always be created for those who receive aid to repay or at
least reciprocate. Even when this cannot be done at once,
the African country receiving aid would wish to preserve
its dignity and retain the right to determine its own policies. Development aid should therefore be regarded as an
expression of a general desire of all nations to accept responsibility for the development of a peaceful world community, marked by mutual respect and tolerance. The
United Nations is expected to encourage these attitudes.

The rejection by Africa of European domination is in part an assertion of racial equality. This is why the African states are unanimous in their denunciation of the apartheid policies of South Africa, or the colonial policies of Portugal at the United Nations. The African challenge to colonial rule, segregation, discrimination, and apartheid asserts that harmonious relations, and consequently world peace, must be based on the recognition of racial equality. It is a challenge which has to be taken seriously, in all its implications. One of these is the demand for social justice. Disabilities and denials of civil liberties based on the biological fact that a man's skin is dark are an affront to all Africans, wherever they are manifested—in South Africa, the United States, France, Portugal or Britain. In this sense, the racial issue properly belongs in the United Nations.

There are some who have recently expressed doubts about the value of the United Nations; some because of the increasing influence of African countries; others, because they fear it is becoming an instrument for carrying out policies of the United States; others again because it is being used by the Soviet Union and its satellites for their own purposes. Whatever the imperfections, there is a clear need for a world body of this kind; for if mankind is to survive, there must be a world body which provides a forum for discussion and opportunities for building a world community. One positive way of building such a community is that of mutual aid and service. The services provided to Africa through the various agencies of the United Nations in many and varied fields—education, health, agriculture, personnel, finance, expert advice, and technical aid—have undoubtedly promoted trust and understanding which are necessary foundations of world peace. UNESCO, ECA, WHO and other United Nations agencies have created faith in the United Nations in

Africa. In combining to help one another, the nations may preserve peace; in separating and refusing to talk, the chances for war are increased. The task is not therefore how to dissolve the United Nations just because the number of African states has increased, or because one nation or another may seek to misuse it, but how to make it truly representative of all the nations of the world, and how to make it more effective for the exchange of views, for international aid and service, and for mutual understanding, based on mutual respect and tolerance of diversity. Within that diversity, African nations, like any other, seek to make their own distinctive contributions to the common heritage of man.

There have been inadequate opportunities and preparation to enable Africans to deal with the social upheavals that have resulted largely from the impact of European technology. Apartheid and various forms of racial discrimination practiced in Africa have denied Africans opportunities of training. It is investment in human resources that is needed most. The most urgent need, and what would perhaps serve the world most beneficially, is for the United Nations through its agencies and organizations to give the peoples of the nations the experience, the skills, and the largeness of heart and mind that are necessary for coping adequately with the problems of our contemporary world. This is a call for giving top priority to investment in man. In some respects, the need for men whose minds and sympathies are large enough for citizenship in a world that is becoming an international community is universal. The United Nations should be an international school for all, and not an instrument manipulated in fratricidal power blocs.

6   A White African Speaks

SIR ROY WELENSKY

SIR ROY WELENSKY, former Prime Minister of the Federation of Rhodesia and Nyasaland (now Northern Rhodesia, Southern Rhodesia, and Malawi), is at present Leader of the Rhodesia Party and is growing fruit, vegetables, and flowers on his 69-acre farm just outside Salisbury. Sir Roy provides a succinct summary of his own career: "My background briefly is that I grew up in the Trade Union movement. I was what you would call an engineer on the footplate, starting as a fireman on the Railways and always a prominent supporter of the Trade Union movement. It was through this movement that I gravitated into politics, eventually ending up as Prime Minister of the Federation, a position I held for seven years until it was finally dissolved by the actions of the British Parliament."

He was made a Companion of the Most Distinguished Order of St. Michael and St. George in 1946 for services during World War II, a Knight Bachelor in Queen Elizabeth's Coronation Honours List of 1953, a Knight Commander of the Most Distinguished Order of St. Michael and St. George in 1959, and a Member of Her Majesty's Privy Council in 1960.

His only book is Welensky's 4,000 Days, *the history of the birth, life, and death of the Federation of Rhodesia and Nyasaland, but he is the subject of two biographies:* The Rhodesian *by Don Taylor and* The Welensky Story *by*

Garry Allighan. He has written for innumerable publica-
tions, and much more has been written about him—in
newspapers, periodicals, and books.

Since the end of World War II Africa has been convulsed
by an ideological revolution which has all but completely
dislodged from the continent the political control formerly
exercised by the colonial powers. This development has
coincided with and been influenced by two other political
factors of great significance, namely the growth of the
United Nations and the Cold War confrontation between
East and West. In the comparatively short period of time
since the United Nations came into existence, its African
membership has grown from four member states to thirty-
three, representing approximately a third of the organization's total membership and a larger contingent than from
any other continent. It is a commonplace that the influence
exercised on world affairs by these independent African
states by virtue of their voting strength in the General Assembly is out of all proportion either to their total population or their financial contribution to the operating costs
of the United Nations. That position will continue to obtain for as long as certain of the major powers base their
foreign policies on respect for or sensitivity to majority
international opinion as expressed through the organs and
agencies of the United Nations, unless of course there is
some radical revision of voting rights, which seems unlikely.

I have mentioned the East–West confrontation as being
a significant factor in this situation. It is significant in the
sense that Russia and her friends, having given aid and
encouragement to political movements which have resulted in the rapid emancipation of African countries from

colonial control in the past few years, are now supporting and indeed inciting the crusading movement amongst African independent nations aimed at "liberating" the remainder of Africa from what they are pleased to call "alien rule." The existence of powerful Western-aligned regimes in southern Africa is clearly an obstacle to international Communist expansion. These regimes, which embrace the Republic of South Africa, the Portuguese Territories of Angola and Mozambique and the self-governing Colony of Southern Rhodesia, must therefore be subverted and overthrown. There is thus a joint Communist–Afro-Asian onslaught on these regimes in southern Africa mounted both within and outside the United Nations.

One might be forgiven for thinking that in these circumstances the countries of the Western Alliance would rally to the defense of their friends in southern Africa. Why in fact is this not so?

There are of course a number of reasons, varying from the sentimental to the coldly practical, and with different emphasis in different countries. Britain and America, of course, are largely influenced by their anxiety to preserve good images with the African, Asian and Latin American countries whose goodwill or supporting votes may be important on crucial international issues. That, of course, is an oversimplification of attitudes but it has enough basic validity to explain why, within limits, the countries of the Western alliance tend to adopt a "me too" position in regard to attacks on southern Africa. As those attacks intensify, they find themselves forced into more and more extreme and uncomfortable positions. Thus by August, 1963, we find Britain and America agreeing respectively to limit and terminate arms supplies to the Republic of South Africa, notwithstanding that South Africa is one of the most important bastions of Western defense in the southern hemisphere. I notice that a former American Ambassador to South Africa, Mr. P. K. Crowe, has called attention to this eccentricity of American policy, making the point that South Africa is "virtually the only sovereign nation in Africa today on whom we could count for a really firm stand against Communist aggression."

I do not intend to set myself up as an advocate of the policies either of our South African or Portuguese neighbors in southern Africa. Their policies are not my policies, and in any case I do not believe in minding other people's business for them. Like Alice in her colloquy with the Duchess, I believe that the world would go round a deal faster if everybody minded his own business, and I sincerely hope that that is a lesson that the world is going to learn before it goes very much further down the slippery slope made up of one United Nations resolution after another condemning this, that or the other thing in some nation's domestic behavior. It is all grossly inconsistent with the United Nations Charter, of course, and it is the purest act of expediency on the part of the Western powers to go along with it. To a degree it is fairly harmless mudslinging but not entirely so, as may be seen from the more recent incursions of the Security Council into the affairs of South Africa and Portugal, for example.

Perhaps the most serious divergence from the principle of noninterference in recent years has been the subjugation of Katanga by the forces of the United Nations despite every pious protestation that they would not be used to impose any political solution in the Congo. We now know that they were cynically used for such a purpose in order that the political objectives of many of the nations backing the U.N. operation might be achieved. So far as Western interests are concerned, it is ironic that the solution which was imposed involved the political extinction of one of the most Western-oriented and capable statesmen in the continent of Africa.[1]

This is the kind of environment in which we are living in Central Africa. Already the pressures round and about us have led to the slow strangulation and death of the Federation of Rhodesia and Nyasaland, a splendid concept in multiracial living and nation-building which in ten short years galvanized into dynamic life the economic possibilities of this area and raised the standard of living of all its inhabitants. All this has been sacrificed to racial intolerance, to the rejection by the black man of white guidance and leadership at this stage of his social, economic and political development. It is the tragedy of impatience.

The retention of white influence in Africa is, of course, a question upon which world opinion is sharply divided. It is perhaps not sufficiently realized that many of our white-skinned Africans have as much claim to permanent domicile in this continent as white-skinned Americans or Australians have in theirs. I have not heard it seriously suggested that the people inhabiting those continents should be repatriated to the homelands of their forebears; or indeed that the Negro population of America should be repatriated to Africa. This is more than a debating point that I am making. There is a common misconception that the white man in Africa is an accidental by-product of the colonial era who must inevitably be washed away when the plug is pulled out of the colonial bath. However valid that may be in relation to certain parts of this continent —and I cannot presume to speak for areas of which I have no personal experience—it has no validity in relation to the Rhodesias, many of whose palefaced inhabitants have lived here for several generations and know no other home.

When I make this point I am not entering some sort of

[1] This was written before the startling reversal which brought Tshombe back to Congolese politics.—Ed.

sentimental plea that the white inhabitants of Central
Africa should be protected on the same basis as royal game.
Their claim to survival on other than purely selfish
grounds rests upon the tremendous contribution that they
have made and will continue to make towards the development of this part of Africa. If the countries of Africa are
to have any hope of closing the gap between their terribly
primitive and depressed conditions and the affluent societies of the Western world it can only be on the basis of
their assimilating the managerial, administrative and technical skills of the Western world and adapting themselves
to a new way of life which will equip them ultimately to
rise to the living standards of the prosperous nations of the
West. It is the white presence in Central Africa that is the
spearhead of the economic breakthrough by which alone
this revolution can take place. No amount of organizational or bilateral aid applied haphazardly here or there is
an adequate substitute for the dynamism of white settlement on the ground, with its capacity for energizing an
expanding and rising economy. The frequently maligned
"white settlers" of Central Africa are not only non-expendable in their own interests; they are non-expendable in the
interests of millions of Africans seeking to live better lives,
and in the interests of the international community at
large—if only it could be made to realize it.

The international community, either separately or cor-
porately through its organizational structure, is ploughing
large sums of money into Africa, either out of a genuine
sense of obligation to an underdeveloped area or out of a
compulsion to buy political goodwill. I have noted an estimate recently that outside aid to Africa was running at a
level of $2 billion in 1961. For later years the figure is
probably substantially higher. This is an expensive commitment. It would be very much more expensive—and very
much less productive in terms of local economic advantage

—if it had to be extended to those areas of Africa whose economic growth is currently sustained by intensive white settlement. At present those areas receive the barest minimum of international handouts; partly because their needs, however great, are not as desperate as the countries which lack the economic stimulus of white settlement; partly because they do not attract political bribery. There is no Cold War political incentive for the United States or any other Western government to channel large-scale aid into Southern Rhodesia, for example. Under its present regime it is staunchly and solidly on the side of the West in the world ideological conflict.

To the extent that American aid flowed into the Federation it flowed mostly in the direction of Nyasaland. That is understandable. As the Territory in the Federation with the smallest white population, Nyasaland (now Malawi) is the poorest and least developed. As the Territory that was the first to leave the Federation to exist independently on its totally inadequate resources, it stands in line to be wooed away from the Eastern embrace.

There are many who, whilst accepting that the case for preserving white influence in Africa is unassailable, maintain that the white man's presence is only tolerable on the black man's terms. This view stems partly from an exaggerated dedication to the concept of counting heads—or "nobbery" as it has been called—and partly from a quite abject capitulation to racial arrogance. In my estimation—and the estimation of a great many of my countrymen—it is no service to anybody to count heads unless you also count what is in them. Full democracy, as the West understands it, is not a sovereign remedy for every political situation, although there is a very widespread tendency for that doctrinaire assumption to be made. Full democracy in the sense of all adult citizens exercising political rights is the end product of a long evolutionary process, of training in citizenship. One of the essential ingredients in this process, of course, is the achievement of a high level of education amongst potential voters. If democracy is to fulfill its purpose the people's choice must be an informed and intelligent choice. If it is not, democracy degenerates into mobocracy and totalitarianism. It has long been a mockery behind the Iron Curtain. It is just becoming so in many of the independent countries of Africa where the tyrannical apparatus of the one-party state has annihilated the values for which democratic man has struggled for centuries— freedom of thought, freedom of speech, and freedom to unseat an unpopular government.

There is a fashionable view that Western democracy does not answer to African needs or temperament and that African countries will inevitably fashion their political institutions on one-party lines. Judged from the standpoint of current developments there is a great deal to support that view. I really have only two points to make about it and they are these: first, do not let us delude ourselves that this new product bears anything but a superficial resemblance to democracy; and secondly, do not expect the quarter-million white Africans in a country like Southern Rhodesia to acquiesce meekly in the extinction of a political and cultural heritage which their forebears have painfully and gloriously hammered out over the centuries. The fact that they are a minority of the population of Southern Rhodesia does not detract from the value of that heritage or from the desirability in human terms of endeavoring to make it more widely shared by people of another race who have not been privileged to enjoy the same inheritance.

Thus it is that those of us who advocate the gradual broadening of the base of political power and responsibility in Central Africa justify our approach by reference on the one hand to material values, that is to say, the maintenance of conditions of rapid economic growth, and on the other hand to spiritual values, that is to say, the preservation of the truly democratic values in our civilization.

It is important to appreciate that what we stand for is meritocracy and not the entrenchment of minority rule. The record of ten years of Federal administration in Central Africa has been the record of the progressive opening up of political, economic and social opportunities to people of all races, with merit as the only criterion. It is true that in Southern Rhodesia political power is still largely concentrated in white hands, but by the ordinary process of evolution that position must change within my lifetime. There are few white men in Southern Rhodesia today who do not accept that change taking place as inevitably as the sun rises in the East. Their principal concern is that when it takes place it will not be accompanied by an overthrow of economic order and progress and of democratic values, as has happened in other parts of Africa.

The philosophy that I have tried to describe is seriously embattled. It is under attack in the United Nations, in the independent countries of Africa and in many influential quarters of the Western world. The motives behind this hostile alignment are not far to seek. They stem primarily from the ideological revolution which has swept through Africa like a bush fire since the end of the Second World War, exciting subject peoples to throw off the yoke of alien rulers. This is not a new phenomenon in the history of the world. American history has its own parallels. A frightening feature of this new revolution, however, is first, that it has become heavily saturated with racialism, and secondly, that it has been able to exploit the Cold War tensions between East and West to extend its aims and objects. Its racial content proceeds from an identification of alien rule with white rule, with the result that what began as an anti-colonial crusade has tended to become an onslaught on white positions everywhere in Africa. Southern Rhodesia is not a colonial situation. It is not subject to alien or distant rule. It is entirely self-governing in all essential respects. It is more truly democratic, subject to the qualifications I have mentioned, than many of the countries which make up the anti-colonial front. The hostility to which it is subjected is attributable to the fact that at this point of time its political and economic power structure is largely in white hands for good and valid historical reasons.

This racial fixation of the anti-colonial forces plays very conveniently into the hands of the Communists. In their struggle for world domination the continent of Africa is an important prize. Before it can be won and exploited it is going to be necessary for Western influence to be eliminated. There are several stages in this process. First, there is the retreat of the colonial power from its position of political control. This in any case is an inevitable and desirable process and there is not likely to be serious disagreement about anything except the timing. There can be very few people who take a responsible view of world affairs who would not accept that the Belgian Government's retreat in the Congo was disastrously precipitate. I am not quite sure what that decision has cost the international community since July, 1960, but it is at least $120 million a year and probably a good deal more. Significantly, Soviet Russia has not contributed towards the cost of retrieving disaster in the Congo. Why should she? The perpetuation of chaos and anarchy serves her interests very much better, being a more fertile breeding ground for Communist ideology.

In November, 1961, the Communist bloc did much to inspire a General Assembly resolution on colonialism which included the words "that inadequacy or political, economic, social or educational unpreparedness should never serve as a pretext for delaying independence." The formulation of the resolution is not in itself remarkable, given the destructive ambitions of the Communist bloc and the impatience of colonial peoples to run their own affairs regardless of the consequences. What is extraordinary is that the resolution was adopted by 97 votes to nil with four abstentions—France, South Africa, Spain and Great Britain. In other words practically every nation in the world, including the United States of America, voted for the view that any colonial dependency should be entitled to its independence regardless of its capacity to govern itself.

By implication—for it must be remembered that this came well after United Nations involvement in the Congo debacle—these nations accepted a responsibility for sorting out at international expense the chaos resulting from the attainment of premature independence. As long as the United States Government and people are prepared to pick up the financial tabs that are left lying around when the colonial power leaves, I suppose that Communist aims will be that much more difficult of accomplishment. I would have thought, however, that there was a limit to the depth of America's pocket and that there were more economical ways of keeping the Russian menace at bay. One of them might be not to kick existing colonial or "settler" influence quite so hard in the pants.

With isolated exceptions there is no remaining colonial situation in Africa as such. So far as questions of political control are concerned, the Communist bloc objective, as we have noted earlier, is to overthrow the regimes in South Africa, Southern Rhodesia, Angola and Mozambique. Until they are removed they are insuperable impediments to a Communist take-over, just as colonial administrations are impediments to a Communist take-over until they are removed. There are signs, I think, that the Communists have a real appreciation of the difficult task they will have in cracking open southern Africa. The Portuguese defenses in Angola have not fallen as easily as some people had supposed; South Africa is an even more formidable proposition.

In the meantime Communist strategy in Africa has moved into a different phase in those parts of the continent which are now subject to the control of indigenous African governments. I think an American statesman has said that what America wants for Africa is what Africans want for themselves. That, of course, is not the case with Russia and her friends. What they want to see in Africa is an extension of Communist ideology and they are working towards that objective by a succession of planned maneuvers. Now that the exercise of colonial political power has been successfully eroded, the Communist challenge is directed against economic influence exercised by the West in the shape of direct aid to African countries or investment in their economies. "Neo-colonialism" is the abusive label attached to Western activities of this kind, and every resource of Communist propaganda will be brought to bear in an attempt to persuade the independent countries of Africa that their independence is a myth and a delusion and that they continue to be subject to exploitation by the imperialistic West. The development of the "neo-colonial" line of attack will be a serious challenge to the West, and particularly to the United States of America, who will find herself in the dock along with the colonial powers, charged with exploiting the peoples of Africa for her own selfish interests. Americans should not delude themselves that it is going to be very much plainer sailing in Africa once the last traces of colonialism and white control have been eliminated. All that will then have happened is that the last positive barriers to Communist subversion will have been dismantled and the field will be wide open for the ideological battle to rage.

I do not pretend to know who is likely to win it, if indeed it should turn out to have a conclusive outcome in East–West terms. What is certain, of course, is that the Communists start with a good many advantages. They are comparative strangers to Africa and do not carry a colonial stigma about with them. The forms of colonial oppression which they themselves apply are too remote and too well guarded against the inquisitive eye ever to have been experienced by Africans. The incitement to revolutionary change is so much more effective when the call is made to people who are barely beginning to emerge from primeval poverty and ignorance. Particularly insofar as the Red Chinese are now actively promoting the Communist line in Africa, there is a non-white racial affiliation that enters into the picture. It is also, of course, very nearly possible for the Communist to say to the African— "Why should you hate me? I have never done anything for you." Certainly the Communist contribution to the needs of Africa has been infinitesimal compared with the contribution from the West.

The response to this challenge will call for the highest qualities of statesmanship. It is not for me to suggest what that response should be, but I am not convinced that it is wise to allow the hungry young nations of Africa to go on hollering for more and more assistance without accepting some obligations of gratitude in return. It might not be a bad thing if some of these young nations were thrown upon the colder charity of Moscow for a while. There might be some salutary comparisons to be made.

Another point I would like to make is in regard to the conclusions of the Conference of African Heads of State that was held at Addis Ababa. It was agreed to establish an Organization of African States as a means of fostering African unity. That in itself, of course, is a highly commendable objective. What is thoroughly objectionable is that the Organization, which has set up a special fund for that purpose, has offered to provide facilities in its members' territories for training in sabotage and subversion, and has generally left little doubt in anybody's mind that there is no length to which member governments will not go to achieve their objective. It is a measure of the double standards to which we have now become accustomed in international affairs that this conspiracy is apparently accepted with equanimity, whilst the domestic affairs of Southern Rhodesia, which incidentally is one of the least troubled territories in Africa, are represented as a threat to international peace and security and quite straight-faced attempts are made to discuss them in the Security Council for that reason. I do not know how long responsible nations are going to accept this ludicrous and hypocritical state of affairs, but I do suggest in all earnestness that the principal donors of aid in Africa ought to consider very seriously whether they are not contributing to an extremely dangerous international situation by continuing to give assistance to nations which make no secret of their intention to devote some of their resources to acts of aggression.

I notice that a distinguished American Africanist, Arnold Rivkin,[2] has referred to "the alarming rate at which scarce capital resources of the new African states are being channeled, frequently with the acquiescence and in some instances with the blessings of donor states, into military expenditure." Mr. Rivkin was speaking prior to the Addis Ababa Conference and he was directing his remarks principally to the economic consequences of the misdirection of resources. My own point, I suggest, gives a special and added significance to Mr. Rivkin's, and I sincerely hope

2 Address to Fourth International Conference of the American Society of African Culture.

that its implications will not be lost upon the Western World.

It may be that the Pan-African aggressors will not be so foolish as to attempt a military adventure against South Africa. If they should do so, however, they will be sternly resisted, and the resulting military confrontation will create a serious international problem. It is in everybody's interest that it should not arise, and I believe it would best be avoided by taking steps to ensure that the potential aggressors do not have the means of aggression at their disposal. The United States Government sees justification in denying military equipment to the Republic of South Africa. I hope she will see equal reason to deny it to members of the Organization of African Unity until such time as they abandon their aggressive postures towards southern Africa. Aggression is an unqualified evil; you cannot have good brands and bad brands. Disapproval of a regime does not justify any attempt to overthrow it by force. I understand that that is a doctrine which the United States Government applies to Cuba; I would expect her to be completely consistent in its application.

So far as the special problems of Southern Rhodesia are concerned, I have referred earlier to the tragedy of impatience, by which I mean of course that so many of the leaders of African opinion are making political claims that white opinion is not prepared at present to concede. These claims are based on the doctrinaire demand for majority rule regardless of its consequences. The white position is more pragmatic. It recognizes that majority rule is natural and inevitable in the long term but that responsibility for guiding the destinies of any nation must be kept in educated and capable hands if administrative and economic efficiency is to survive, together with the values of a democratic society. I think it is important for the world to realize, first, that the white position in Southern Rhodesia is to protect standards and not privilege; second, that the white man's determination to protect the values of his society is not likely to be eroded by cajolery, bullying or abuse from outside his borders, particularly from quarters which cannot offer unblemished records either of governmental competence or of democratic virtue. The effect of such behavior is far more likely to drive the white man into defensive obstinacy, especially if it is accompanied by uncritical acclaim of the accomplishments of majority-rule conditions elsewhere in Africa which are clearly recognizable as unconvincing. There may be grounds for arguing that the white man should be prepared to concede a little further and faster to the natural aspirations of the black man. Unfortunately there is far too much emphasis in the world today on the proposition that he should concede all now and hope for the best. I am afraid that the best that he sees around him is not good enough either in terms of efficiency or democratic morality. It is high time that some pressures were applied the other way and that African leadership was called upon to show more patience and more willingness to compromise. There is, after all, nothing particularly evil about oligarchies or, as I prefer to call them, meritocracies, provided they are based, as ours is in Southern Rhodesia, on talent, and provided they are moving towards a fuller concept of democracy. Most of the flourishing democracies of Western Europe have developed in that way. We can do worse than follow the same paths in Africa.

7 An Outside Observer Speaks

THOMAS MOLNAR

THOMAS MOLNAR, *born in Budapest in 1921, is now an American citizen and a Professor of French Literature at Brooklyn College. He holds an M.A. in French Literature and in Philosophy from the University of Brussels and a Ph.D. from Columbia University. He recently spent six months traveling in Africa from the Mediterranean to the Cape, on a grant from the Relm Foundation.*

He is the author of Bernanos, His Political Thought and Prophecy, The Future of Education, The Decline of the Intellectual, *and* The Two Faces of American Foreign Policy. *His new book will be entitled* Africa, A Political Travelogue.

Dr. Molnar is New York correspondent for L'Esprit Public *and* La France Catholique *in Paris and a regular contributor to* National Review *and* Modern Age. *He also writes for other European and American periodicals.*

To a large extent Africa today is a continent of make-believe, illusion and assumption. The decolonization process is wrapped in a cloak of self-righteousness and utopianism: on the one hand, it is suggested that the colonizing white man has been guilty of retarding the development

132

of Africa; on the other hand, it is assumed that, emancipated finally, the black man is going to create a paradise
on earth.

These clichés, encouraged by large sections of the Western press and by debates in the United Nations, not only
simplify but falsify the true picture. Without going into
the history of African colonization, and into the sad and
bloody state of affairs the white man found on his arrival,
one can see, while traveling in Africa, the enormous
achievements of the last hundred years or so—achievements
entirely of the colonial period: cities and towns with orderly streets and public security; administrative systems,
and a judicial system now preferred by Africans to their
traditional tribal justice; irrigation systems, modern agricultural methods, and assistance to farmers and peasants;
excellent and well-staffed hospitals and schools; the beginnings of secondary industry. Generally speaking, conditions of security have replaced a state of affairs in which
tribes massacred each other and villagers could not leave
the vicinity of their huts alone without exposing themselves to kidnaping, rape, or armed attack by men of the
neighboring village.

We may then safely say that the colonial period has been
an integral and, let us hope, organic part of the history of
the newly emerging African countries. I say "organic part,"
because, unless the new governments are ready to build on
what has already been achieved, they face chaos, disintegration, and a long period of demagogy and decline. It
must be stressed that what the traveler sees today in Africa
is still a "Europeanized" continent, certainly in its urban
centers, but even in the countryside and in the forests, for
white influence has reached the most remote recesses of
native life. The real problem of decolonization is, then,
whether the present can be stabilized and further improved, or whether occult influence will prevail and the

temptation of indolence prove stronger than the efforts needed for civilizing work.

Does this mean that the new African countries must imitate and copy everything white or Western? Not in theory, since African mentality and inventiveness, culture and customs, are realities in their own right. But practically, the situation is this: in spite of the emerging African consciousness, in spite of the *négritude* of which the French-speaking Africans are so proud, the black man has a deep-seated admiration for the white man. When the Tunisian contingent arrived in the Congo under United Nations command, the Congolese asked the soldiers how long Tunisia had been independent. Since 1956, was the answer. "That then is why your skin is lighter than ours," said the Congolese. In other words, independence, freedom, the amenities of modern life are associated in the average black man's mind with the white man's qualities, with whiteness. Thus it is idle to ask to what extent the African countries are going to try to create states on the Western model: they will and they must create such states if they want to remain states at all. For the alternative is not merely a differently conceived state and nation, but—given Africa's past and the black man's racial tradition—falling back on tribalism, anarchy, and misery. In Africa, concretely as well as figuratively speaking, the jungle, the sand and the savanna are always present and they threaten to engulf and annihilate what man has created. The white man's historic contribution to life on that continent was to show the way these ever-present dangers may be eliminated or at least kept at a safe distance. The new Africa has no choice but to follow in the white man's footsteps. And, of course, this is exactly what the black leaders say they want: improved agricultural methods, organization of modern industry, widespread education, smooth administration. And they

say it in English, French or Afrikaans, trying to adapt the
European terms to their native languages and concepts.

The question is, what are the chances for success of this
vast enterprise? What is the positive side of decolonization
and how permanent does it promise to be?

The popular concept holds that "colonialism" is the exploitation and unjust treatment of the black man by the
white man. I pointed out earlier that "colonialism" is also,
and in the long run more importantly, the creation of a
network of civilization which will have to be the foundation of all further progress in Africa. But we should not
underestimate the popular concept either: colonialism did
mean and still does mean in many parts of Africa, exploitation and, if no longer bad treatment, at least psychological
and moral humiliation of the black by the white. Most
white Africans dismiss this aspect of the coexistence of
races with one or more of the following arguments: there
is also a black racism and mistreatment of black man by
black man; the black men are in such a vast majority that
unless the white man dictates the rules, he will be sub-
merged, his work undone, he himself driven out or worse;
it would be unjust to make exceptions in favor of an educated minority of black men and admit them, and them
only, to equal rights with the white men; the black man
does not really want to mix with the whites, he feels more
at home with his own people; and so on.

These arguments, based in part on truth, are, however,
largely false: in every part of Africa I found that the black
man keenly feels the humiliation of his situation, and more
so, naturally, when he is educated and cultured. In that
part of Africa previously administered by France the situation in this respect is best: French policy has always been
to favor brilliant students, steep them in French culture
and manners, and accept them as equal or very nearly
equal. (The reverse side of this policy is that the French-

educated black men have acquired the habits and terminology of French political ideology and have transplanted
them to African soil where they produce grotesque results.
But this is another question.)

In Belgian and British Africa the black man was definitely kept in a position of inferiority. Before the Belgians'
departure, a native could not reach even minor administrative positions, let alone be accepted in the professions.
In British East Africa or Rhodesia the black man could
be educated to a high degree, but no less discriminated
against than his less fortunate fellow African. A prosperous
businessman in Salisbury, one of the fifteen black members
of the Parliament, told me as we were sitting in his villa:
"The whites have cheated us: they had promised that the
educated African would be socially promoted, which
meant also that we, the elite, could have told our people
that education is the highway to their own promotion too.
This would have offered an avenue of opportunity; we no
longer would have felt hopelessly blocked in our ambitions. Instead of this, I, a member of parliament, cannot
go to a white restaurant and ask for a beer. Members of my
race, whoever they may be, are simply not served."

It must be understood, and unfortunately many white
Africans do not understand it, that in black society there
is the same desire of the well-to-do and of the educated to
distinguish themselves from the poor and uneducated as
in white society; the wound of humiliation inflicted on
Mr. Gondo (the deputy in Salisbury) is as deep as it would
be on any European in similar circumstances.

In South Africa, in many respects an admirable country,
discrimination has been erected into a system, with the absolute and rigid logic of the white man unchecked by any
other considerations. The black and white races are completely different, the partisans of apartheid say, they do not
want to mix, they wish to follow different cultural paths.

Let us keep them separated: at entrances to buildings, in the elevators, in the post office, on park benches, everywhere except in the streets and workshops. The white South Africans forget that it is precisely the streets with their automobiles, Western-dressed people and bright shop windows, and the workshops with their technical precision and Western planning, which give the Bantus the desire not only to imitate the white man but also to mix with him. I had a long conversation about this problem with Mr. Abraham, General Commissioner of the Xhosa nation in the newly created Transkei, west of Natal. Like most of those white South Africans who have responsibility for native affairs, Mr. Abraham is a deep-thinking man, a realist, a man who devotes his life to the well-being of the natives. Yet, also like most of the people in these positions, his thinking has an incorrigible flaw. He argued with me that all the Bantus want (the collective name "Bantu" includes Zulus, Xhosas, Sotos, Tembus, etc.) they can find in their own reserves. "They are attracted to the white towns by the movies, the lemonade and the Western-type clothing," Mr. Abraham said. "If we guarantee them these things in their own native townships, they will not want to come among the whites any more." This theory is characteristic of white logic in many areas of Africa; for such white men, decolonization can be achieved simply by separating blacks from whites, granting the former material well-being and self-government, but otherwise maintaining the two juxtaposed communities under a system of economic cooperation.

A similar theory prevails, with certain variations, in the Portuguese territories of Angola and Mozambique. The Portuguese insist that all the "assimilados" among the black men—that is those who have achieved a degree of education and white civilization—are of equal rank with similarly advanced Portuguese white men, whereas the uneducated and undeveloped, black and white, can have no full rights as voters, etc. But all Angolians and Mozambicans, irrespective of race, are considered Portuguese. I witnessed, for example, a touching scene while visiting the Sao Nicolau penal camp for the toughest of Holden Roberto's terrorists. Captured by Portuguese forces and condemned to a maximum of four years, they are treated far more mildly than convicts in any Western prison would be. Indeed, they live in little stone houses with their families; their children go to school with the Commandant's children; and the prisoners themselves work on the plantation, sharing on a fifty-fifty basis the produce of their work with the government which provides for their needs. As we were driving around in a Land Rover, we came upon a group of children playing under the supervision of two adults (ex-terrorists). They greeted us, and the Commandant suggested that they sing the Portuguese national hymn. The Commandant listened to the singing with tears in his eyes, and said to me as we bade good-bye to the little group: "You see, these people, the terrorists included, are good Portuguese. We must forgive them because they were misled by outsiders."

Mr. Abraham and Captain Pegado are examples of white men who with excellent intentions are firmly executing a plan designed to do justice to the natives. What they do not understand is the crucial fact that the natives want to be independent, because at a certain stage of development people want to look after their own business. Does it mean that the natives of Angola or South Africa have a clear consciousness of their *négritude* or even of their independent Angolan or Bantu nationality? Except for a very small minority, these natives have no such consciousness and most probably do not care whether they are called Portuguese or Angolan, Bantu or South African. While today the majority of them accept the label the white man gives them, tomorrow they will accept a new label with the same docility. Decolonization and independence are in the consciousness of a minority; but movements in history are always propelled by minorities.

We may safely conjecture that the present fever of inde-pendence in Africa is not an artificially created agitation, but a genuine idea. This does not mean, as Western "pro-gressive" circles like to allege, that independence "had to come because the wind of history was blowing in that di-rection." This is utterly false, and in a sense it would have been better for all concerned if independence had come more gradually. At the risk of simplification it may be said that independence came so swiftly because the United States was pressing its wartime allies to contribute to the "better world" that seems to have been the objective of Washingon's foreign policy since Wilson and Roosevelt. And it came even more swiftly than Washington had imag-ined because the United Nations, an insatiable body, needed to strengthen itself with the addition of new limbs, no matter how weak and wobbly.

Whatever the origin and rate of the decolonization proc-ess, the independent states are here to stay—and to pose extraordinary problems, the end of which is not in sight. These countries live at present on the moral capital of their accumulated grievances against the Western world; I said above that these grievances are real enough, although they are more than compensated by the accomplishments the white man leaves behind. At any rate, one cannot con-tinue to live on past suffering and one cannot indefinitely demand exceptional treatment on that basis. The real ques-tion is then whether, now that independence and sov-ereignty are achieved, these countries will be able to survive and prosper by dint of their own resources, skill, and state-building abilities.

Certain people and news organs in the West, prone to

the easy demagogic statement, enthusiastically declare that
there is no difference between the races, that all are capable of the same effort, that being decolonized is in itself a
kind of special virtue. Briefly, they seem to argue that
merely to ask the question whether Mali or Ghana might
become a state, and a modern state at that, is an insult
"enlightened world opinion" cannot tolerate. Yet, this
question *must* be asked if we are concerned with the future
of Africa and of the world. The elements of the answer one
is able to give at this point are three in number: the opinion of the black men, that of the white men who were born
or have lived and worked in Africa, and the personal observations, however limited, of the traveler from outside.

Let us begin with the last point, perhaps the most un-
certain of the three. I have said that observing Africa at
present is observing the work of the white man in planning,
conceiving, carrying it out. Thus, literally, we cannot *know*
what the Africans are capable of in terms of their obvious
objective, the creation of states on the Western model and
on the lines of Western efficiency. We see magnificent
presidential palaces, but they were built for the French,
English, Belgian, colonial governor; we see proud airlines,
but the planes were manufactured in the West and are
piloted by Western pilots; we live in beautiful hotels, but
under Western management; we walk on well-lined ave-
nues with comfortable apartment buildings, but they were
designed by foreign architects; we deal with banks, postal
systems, stores and shops, but they still run on organizational lines devised by the ex-colonial and he is still the
moving, directing force behind them; we have delightful
conversations with black-skinned ministers and officials
about their future plans for such and such departments,
but their subalterns and directors are still white and run
the administration in old and tested ways.

To mention these things is not to slight the African; but

the life of a society, of a nation, is not a plaything with which one may take chances. And the alarming fact is that in many parts of Africa signs of mismanagement, indolence and irresponsibility are already apparent. Let us add here immediately that one reason is the gradual pulling-out of the white element. Whether because they refuse to work under black authority, or because they no longer feel safe, or because they see no future for their children, the fact is that the white men are leaving. And when they remain, even when they return, one has the clear impression that they have one hope: to make quick money, to liquidate existing assets, and then depart definitively.

Thus the beginning of black management is often marred by the absence, near-absence, or half-hearted presence of continuity. It is disturbing to realize that much too often the traveler's impressions are confirmed by the local white man's elaborately expressed views on Africa. To sum up these impressions, I should say that where the white man is no longer present, there comes in his place a subtle disintegration, indolence, *je m'enfoutisme*. The buildings are not cared for, the sidewalks become indistinguishable from the pavement, public works decay, idling crowds settle in unexpected places, the rhythm of civilized life slows down, time loses its importance. The black man still goes through the motions inculcated by the white man: police, mail, hygiene, etc. are still functioning; but somehow it seems that only shadows persist that might vanish tomorrow. All this creates a feeling of unreality and often of outright *malaise*. To give an example: after spending some weeks in Angola where everything is spotless, well-organized, smoothly running, I visited the Léopoldville headquarters of Holden Roberto's liberation movement. The young leaders I talked to were intelligent, acute-minded people who had grandiose dreams of an independent, modern Angolan state. But when I looked around, the dirt, the broken furniture, the filthy rooms, the sticky objects, and last but not least the idle young men and women sitting or lying on the floor or in the dust were appalling. How can these people think of running a modern state or the brightly lit, lovely Luanda, Angola's capital, when they do not even attempt to live in decent surroundings, to clean up the filth, to use a couple of buckets of water (there were plenty of people around to do it) to wash the most obvious eyesores? Poverty is, of course, no excuse, for these people get enough aid from outside to run an insurrectionary movement and a guerrilla war. It is not a question of funds, but of brooms and buckets.

Thus it is that the local white men, even when they see rays of hope, usually outline a rather gloomy prospect. I want to mention here that throughout my three and a half months of travel in Africa I insisted on interviewing people in a wide variety of fields and professions: priests, professors, trade unionists, radio directors, farmers, workers, politicians, lawyers, doctors, housewives, librarians, journalists, police officials, plantation owners, judges, technical advisors, United Nations personnel, students. It would be impossible for me simply to exclude the views expressed by these people (I am now speaking of whites only) who have lived, in many cases all their lives, in contact with African realities and with black neighbors.

Their criticism of the African, which naturally colors their predictions for the Africans' future, may be divided into three categories: agriculture, political life, and general mentality.

Agriculture is decisive, because the main, the urgent problem of the continent is food supply and the improvement of a still predominantly agrarian way of life. When the white man came, the cultivation of land was extremely elementary, since in Africa nobody will starve if he lives off the forests and what grows naturally. But cattle are considered most important; they are used in place of cash, they are a status symbol, and they constitute the dowry for buying wives. Grazing is therefore ubiquitous; the topsoil erodes because of over-cultivation, insufficient use of fertilizers, and the chopping down of entire forests for firewood. In subtropical and equatorial Africa cultivation would require great and sustained efforts in any case; the heat is such that it speeds up chemical reactions in the soil and scarcely permits cultivation of staple vegetables or wheat. It is of course excellent for plantations of coffee, cocoa and banana, but such plantations must be run with extreme care and considerable capital. The result is that the land that the white man occupies, even if it was not of better quality at the beginning than the land occupied by the black man, yields more, is more rationally exploited, produces more varied products, allows greater investment. In order to change the black man's ancient ways of cultivation, his entire mode of living and customs will have to be changed: his fields fenced off from grazing cattle and terraced when they are on a hillside, different crops experimented with, and other innovations made. The tribal structure of land property hardly makes room for such methods, and often when one farmer fares better than his neighbor, the latter's envy takes violent forms.

Add to this the admirable, but ultimately ruinous custom (one should say, tribal law) that an African is not allowed to turn away from his door members of his family and tribe when they are in need. Thus the more prosperous farmer (but also the more prosperous city dweller, even when he becomes a Minister) never has enough money since he must feed a large and undefined number of people. Tribal and family solidarity is such that many people do not work simply because they can count on the generosity of another. In summary, the individualistic spirit, for better or worse, is not developed in the African; and even when individual peasants are willing to accept state-offered free advice and even free grain and the assistance of agronomists, it is sufficient for this advice to prove wrong once for the farmer to become suspicious for a long time to come. Among the examples quoted to me was that of a farmer who was persuaded to try planting cotton; the following year there was a dip in world market prices, from which he concluded that there were malevolent advisers at work.

Examples could be multiplied, and not only with regard to agriculture. In the eyes of white critics they point up the extreme slowness of transforming the ways of thinking of the African and would justify another fifty years of white presence in Africa, meaning by this white authority and paternalism. Of course, the transformation *is* taking place: whether in South Africa or newly independent Kenya, white and black economists are trying to awaken in the black farmer what they call "cash consciousness," to have him limit the number of his beasts, fence off his fields, experiment with crops. In both countries, for example, meat-packing factories are built in order to tempt the farmer to slaughter his cattle and receive cash for the meat. I want to stress here that since this problem is Africa-wide, both black and white governments look for basically the same solutions, and there is no one who would intentionally retard them. But the whites emphasize the difficulty involved, the gap that is likely to remain between white and black cultivators, whereas the black politicians claim that under their own guidance the people will be willing to adopt new methods. In conclusion, the whites say: "We need more time to improve the level of the Africans"; the blacks answer: "Give us independence, we can do it right now."

But of course they cannot do it right now (whereas the

whites would always ask for more time). The reason is that not even they could change overnight the tribal traditions and superimpose a modern state-structure on the ancient way of life and political concepts. Much has been written about African tribalism, its strength and weakness: the whites usually stress its strength, implying that a modern state composed of black men is not viable, it must eventually disintegrate and fall back on the basic political reality of the black race, the tribe. Hence in South Africa the government makes every possible effort to strengthen the tribal chiefs, tribal justice, tribal living together. In the newly formed Transkei there is a minority of elected members in Parliament, while the majority consist of tribal chiefs who are ex-officio members—and who, after all, have the experience of leadership.

The black politicians of the new countries assert, on the contrary, that tribalism would set their people back, prevent the formation of a modern state, and dissolve a barely achieved national unity. As Mr. Mwai Kibaki, bright young Minister of Economic Planning of Kenya, told me in Nairobi, the state is the twentieth-century form of authority. In Africa, he added, it is bound to take the place of tribal authority, which was democratic in the sense that it was—it still is—based on general consensus against which no chief would ever think of acting.

It is difficult to decide who is right. It is true that the tribal relationship is still extremely strong, and it is no less true that tribal warfare still exists. Underneath the Congo crisis there is tribal antagonism; the Portuguese in Angola use Southern tribes to combat the Northern supporters of Holden Roberto; in Kenya the Masai distrust the Kikuyus and Jomo Kenyatta, who is a Kikuyu; in Southern Rhodesia the warlike Matabeles have sent word to the government that if it contemplates passing rule to the majority (which would be the Mashonas, traditional enemies of the Matabele), they will start preparing for war; in South Africa the Bantus are fighting among themselves (I have mentioned that they consist of at least a dozen tribes and nations) and, incidentally, would massacre the 400,000 Indians in the country if the white police did not stand by.

On the other hand, the black politicians argue that these antagonisms are largely a result of the white policy of divide-and-rule. This is false. But it is true that tribalism is considerably weakened whenever it comes in contact with modern urban life. As in other parts of the world, there is an irresistible migration from the countryside toward the towns. Engulfed by city life, the young African gets detached from the tribe, sometimes even from his immediate family. This phenomenon is the same in black-governed countries as in South Africa. The manpower is needed, and it is almost impossible to tell the black worker (as it was difficult to tell the European or American worker in the nineteenth century) to go back to the land and in this instance the tribal way of life.

It cannot, of course, as yet be proved whether black governments are better able to channel the masses and solve the agricultural and urban problems than are white ones. To gain more firm authority and not be hampered by opposition parties (behind which he sees the forces of tribalism), the emerging African leader, whether his name is Kenyatta, Banda, Nkrumah, Houphouët-Boigny or Kaunda, wants to set up a one-party state. This has its advantages but also its dangers. René Dumont, certainly no enemy of African independence, pointed up in his book, *L'Afrique Noire est mal partie,* the widespread corruption and power-hungry irresponsibility in governing circles. But even if this were not the case, there are reasons to believe that it is not easy for a native government to be accepted by its people. They often prefer to be commanded by whites, and more often than not trust the white (administrator, doctor, judge) more than their fellow-African. In turn, relatively few Africans are dedicated to devotion to members of their race when they could help them concretely, not just with high-sounding statements. It is quite true that it is the white doctor, not the black, who devotes his life to setting up a sanitary station in the thick of the jungle; and, whatever the reason, it is also true that the black man, when he chooses a profession, or gets into high position, becomes a harsh master to members of his own race.

Another important aspect of political life in the future of Africa is the problem of multiracial societies. Africa is not only black; each of the new states consists of citizens of several races: white, Indian, Arab, "colored," and others. The general assumption is that once colonial rule is terminated, racial antagonism will automatically disappear from the continent, because racialism is a one-way street: white discrimination against non-whites. This is, of course, another indication that Africa today is largely a continent of make-believe. There are racial conflicts practically everywhere in Africa, and they are likely to assert themselves precisely with the disappearance of white domination. Black men are "racists" by the same token as others are. The Indians in South Africa would be in danger of their lives, and certainly of their livelihood, if black domination were established in that country; the Mau-Mau of Kenya chose its victims among the Asian minority also; there is no love lost between Arab and black, the blacks openly admitting their antipathy and the Arabs not concealing their contempt; events in Zanzibar showed recently that, in spite of the common bond of Moslem religion, the black man's revolt was directed against the Arab merchant class which previously exploited him; in the Congo there is open fear that the Indians, under cover of United Nations' operations, are penetrating that land with a view to securing a privileged position.

Anti-colonialism is thus but one aspect of a general awakening of the black men to the possibility of taking over the continent, at least its sub-Saharan part. The term "Africanization" assumes, in many instances, the meaning of "negrization," of black take-over. A significant example of what is happening is the case of Kenya. The government, upon achieving independence, decreed that outside of those who were born in Kenya, and who automatically become citizens (in the case of non-blacks, however, at least one parent's Kenyan birth must also be proved), all present residents must apply for citizenship within two years if they wished to stay in the country. During the first month, only *two hundred* non-blacks, that is whites and Indians, applied out of a combined white and Indian community of *two hundred thousand!* As leaders of the Indian community admit, although the Indians, unlike the whites, have nowhere else to go ("India is too crowded," they say), they still hesitate, defenseless as they are, to expose themselves to the risks of becoming citizens—meaning second-class citizens—of a black state. This hesitation, in turn, irritates Kenya's leaders who see in it a lack of confidence in their fairness and in Kenya's future. The more outspoken among them already insist that "Africanization" should mean that *black* Africans take over all the important positions. Again, perhaps nobody is to be blamed for this racial jealousy and mistrust, but they do not augur well for the creation of multiracial societies.

The third *caveat* that white observers of emerging Africa enter may be described as a general skepticism concerning the black man's ability to run a twentieth-century type society. Much of this skepticism may be ascribed to bitterness in seeing their life-work handed over to those whom they used to rule. Much of it, however, is genuine and apparently justified. After half an hour's conversation the African white man will tell you that basically one never knows what is in the black man's mind. This is not a sign of lack of interest, for every African white with whom I talked, without a single exception, is passionately concerned with the black man, I would even say obsessed with him. Their long existence side by side would be sufficient to explain this concern, but there is more: the white man's curiosity, his stubbornness in the face of an enigma. The black man's mentality *is* an enigma to the white who, for want of a more plausible explanation, attempts for the traveler a behavioral analysis. This analysis is so strikingly identical all over the continent that it is difficult not to pay some attention to it.

The African is a showman (the exposé runs) who loves to use words for the sake of hearing himself speak, of making an impression, and of pleasing his momentary listener. But there is little conviction underneath, and even less political thinking or ideological faith. This is, by the way, why Communism has no future in Africa since the black man does not seriously commit himself, but rather exploits the advantages a situation offers. Thus religious beliefs are equally superficial, and many people predict that with the departure of the whites, Christianity will suffer numerically among the blacks, too many of whom will abandon it for the sake of something more opportune, for example, Islam.

The African, the whites maintain, makes and adjusts rules to suit him best. Since he lived long under the Western system, he adopted temporarily the terms of this system and, since he is a born actor and orator, he uses them with a superb skill. But the time was not sufficient for Western influence and a Western milieu to make a deeper penetration of the African's soul. Hence, the white observers conclude, the African remains basically unreliable, selfish; he never practices abnegation, does not know the meaning of self-sacrifice. His main motivation is envy and the desire to be applauded, to be popular. When one argues that there are a number of brilliant black Africans whose insights, reasoning power, and cultural horizon place them in the highest category, the answer is that there are too few of them, and that they will be absorbed, before others might join their number, in a kind of new primitivism which is the likely future for Africa.

This controversy puts the spotlight on the problem of education, considered in the twentieth century as a universal panacea. There is a tremendous desire in the young African today to become educated, to attend high schools and universities, to make any sacrifice in order to obtain the much-coveted diploma. The blacks say that more education will solve practically all their problems: manpower shortage, industrial competence, national and democratic consciousness. The whites, as I pointed out before, tend to believe that the Africans will choose non-productive branches of education through which, however, positions of prestige might be secured. This disagreement will ultimately be decided by future facts. For the time being one might heed the opinion of academic personnel presently operating in African universities like those of Dakar, Abidjan (not yet complete), Lovanium near Léopoldville, the Bantu College at Turfloop in South Africa, the University College in Salisbury. The white professors at these schools see no distinction between white and black students; in fact, since the latter's background and home life are decidedly less developed in most cases, they tend to ascribe extra merit to the tenacity and achievements of black students. As Rector Potgieter of Turfloop Bantu College told me (incidentally, South African universities for the natives are not "façades" but serious institutions of learning), the "black student's basic motivation is no less the search for truth than is the white student's." This view was confirmed by professors of all these institutions.

It is, I think, evident from the above examination of Africa today that in every domain—agriculture, tribal customs, education—a controversial picture emerges. In the present world atmosphere only one side of this picture is, in the main, stressed—namely, the evils of colonialism and thus by definition the virtues and merits of the ex-colonial peoples. Yet the other side should be discussed too in order to obtain a balanced view between the present *facts* and the future *hopes*. It seems to me not too adventurous to say that the black Africans lack many of the qualities which go into the building of modern, efficient, well-administered societies, particularly when, as is the case in the new nations of Africa, they also lack a healthy economic understructure. Tenacity, drive, persistence, reliability, and an individualistic spirit (which is, however, compatible with a sense of responsibility) are disturbingly absent. It may be that this is due to decades of white rule and paternalism; but it may also be due to racial and social characteristics.

The best immediate solution would be a continuing white presence until the new states are securely on their own feet. But, as I have said before, this is not likely to be accepted by the members of either community. The demagogic accusation against the remaining whites of "neocolonialism" is not reassuring; where white advisers are chosen by black chiefs of state (as in the Ivory Coast or Congo-Brazzaville under Fulbert Youlou), the black leaders are accused of favoritism, of having sold out to the white men, and the white advisers themselves are surrounded with envy and jealousy. Some so-called "international-minded" individuals suggest that the personnel of international or technical agencies, like the United Nations, or the Peace Corps, might take over advisership from the ex-colonial whites; but it is enough to spend even a short time in Africa to realize that such personnel, without roots in this very complex soil, without commitment growing out of deep knowledge of the local conditions and mentality, and especially without authority, can never impress the African, can never awaken in him the will to improve his lot.

For the time being, at least, there is no answer to the problems of Africa, no reassuring answer, that is. Does this mean that the continent is bound to sink in despair and primitivism? It would not be hard to find many people who reach just this conclusion. But Africa is an enormous land, and no generalization may be entirely valid, not even when only black Africa is considered. The probability is that most countries will limp along, almost constantly on the brink of bankruptcy, interrupted by somewhat more favorable periods, but always attached to the strings of mightier industrial powers of the Western world. Only large-scale industry could provide the needed stabilizing element; but anyone who has seen Africa knows that industrialization, if it ever comes, will remain very modest indeed, somewhat haphazardly created and often for prestige purposes, and in any case dependent for machinery, spare parts, and supplies on Western suppliers.

When one considers the future of Africa, it is instructive to visit the two countries which have never been colonies. Both were independent and one of them is very ancient; Liberia and Ethiopia. In most respects, they are far more backward than the ex-colonial countries. Dakar, Abidjan, Léopoldville, Nairobi, are big modern cities; Addis Ababa is an aggregate of a few haphazardly erected modern buildings almost lost among vast slums, with villages of huts and pastures right by the side of fifteen-story hotels. The city-dwellers of Kenya, Senegal, the Congo, show white influence in their way of life, and they would not be out of place on the streets of Western capitals; the Ethiopians, a

charming, polite, smiling people, often seem like cave-
dwellers, who look at white tourists as if they were a
strange breed—an indication of the traditional absence of
contact with Western influence, habits and ideas. I am not
here judging the ways of Ethiopia; I am only stating that
lack of contact—hence also of colonial contact—with white
civilization is a factor contributing to stagnation, when, I
repeat, the African objective *is* to catch up with the modern, Western world.

The danger facing the new countries of the continent
then is that of regressing to the stage of the least developed
among them.

FOCUS

ON THE INCANDESCENT TIP

8 The Complexities of South Africa

W. H. HUTT

WILLIAM HAROLD HUTT *was born in 1889 and educated in* London. *He served in the R.F.C. and R.A.F. from 1917 to 1919. Later he studied at the London School of Economics. He worked for a few years in a London publishing house before entering academic life at the University of Cape Town in 1928. In 1931 he was appointed Professor of Commerce and Dean of the Faculty of Commerce and held this post until his retirement at the end of 1964.*

He is the author of several books on theoretical and applied economics, including The Theory of Idle Resources *(1939),* Plan for Reconstruction *(1943),* Keynesianism—Retrospect and Prospect *(1963) and* The Economics of the Colour Bar *(1964).*

Other major contributions of his have appeared as articles. His "The Factory System of the Nineteenth Century" (1926) was republished in 1954 in Hayek's Capitalism and the Historians, *and his "Theory of Collective Bargaining" (1930) was republished in 1954. His 1954 article, "The Significance of Price Flexibility," was reprinted in Hazlitt's* The Critics of Keynesian Economics *(1960), and in 1955 he contributed an article, "The Yield from Money Held," to a symposium in honor of economist Ludwig von Mises,* On Freedom and Free Enterprise *(edited by Sennholz).*

In condemning the "apartheid" policy (more recently termed "separate development") of the Republic of South Africa, the world is passing judgment upon a situation which, I believe, it usually fails to understand. There are obvious aspects of that policy of which no humanitarian could approve; and yet those who express disapproval seldom show any realistic insight into the political and economic setup which has created the non-Whites' grievances. Through this lack of understanding, the condemnatory attitudes commonly adopted towards South Africa, whether through the United Nations or otherwise, are often both unjust and injudicious. This essay is an attempt at a very brief explanation of the problems which arise in an ethnically complex society in which there are about three million Whites (about 60 percent Afrikaans-speaking and 40 percent English-speaking), eleven million Africans, one and a half million "Coloureds" (half-castes) and half a million Indians.

During the regime of the Dutch East India Company in the Cape in the seventeenth and eighteenth centuries, a society emerged in which slaves and very primitive natives (chiefly Hottentots) provided the greater part of the manual labour. The ideas and customs which crystallized during this period survived the abolition of slavery by the British (in 1834); they were perpetuated by the natural rigidity of the minds of men, and they were fortified by the religious teachings of the Calvinistic Dutch Reformed Church of South Africa. In consequence, the strength of fashion and tradition alone confined those whose skin happened not to be white to fields in which they could be hewers of wood and drawers of water. Even in the Cape (as distinct from the Orange Free State and Transvaal Republic, to which many Afrikaners trekked after the abolition of slavery), although nineteenth century liberalism had some considerable influence upon colour attitudes, and although the Coloured people became enfranchised, the non-Whites remained almost entirely a labouring and socially inferior class.

But with the discoveries of diamonds and gold, foreign resources flowed in and a modern "capitalist" regime began slowly to emerge. At once forces were released which *tended* to set in train a disintegration of the customary outlook. It is a characteristic of the private enterprise system that it creates incentives for entrepreneurs to serve society by discovering and utilizing the least-cost methods of producing the things which the community demands. In trying to secure profits (and avoid losses), they are led to search for underutilized, underdeveloped resources; and in South Africa the most seriously underdeveloped resources were the powers of the non-White people. Hence emergent capitalism introduced powerful egalitarian pressures expressed through the colour-blind free market. For even the white people have failed to ask, when purchasing a commodity, "Was this made by a white man or a black man?" Their sole interest has been, "Is it good value for money?"

The private enterprise system is almost universally reproached because it tends, sometimes quite ruthlessly, to dissolve privilege, including colour privilege. Insofar as this system has not been repressed, it can be observed always to have raised, firstly the material standards of the poorer classes and races [1] and then, in consequence, the social respect in which they have been held. The difficulty is that the dissolution of privilege inevitably threatens the relative status (and sometimes the absolute standards) of formerly powerful classes. We find therefore the emergence of counterpressures to the egalitarian influence of competitive capitalism. These counterpressures, which we can describe by the broad terms socialism or leftism, aim at curbing the process by which entrepreneurs ferret out

[1] Unless population growth has not perpetuated the former poverty.

underutilized human capacity, train it, and employ it; and in South Africa these counterpressures have taken the form of colour bars.

The colour bars in South Africa can be classified under seven broad categories.

(1) Incomparably the most powerful colour bar has been "the standard wage rate," *i.e.*, "the rate for the job." Minimum wage rates were originally fixed through private coercion exerted by labour unions, but later they were imposed by the state as part of the "civilized labour policy," mainly through the Wage Act (1925) and the Industrial Conciliation Act (1924). By preventing the non-Whites from discounting the prejudice against employing them, from discounting their initial inferiority of background and education, and from discounting the additional costs of employing them (due to the hostility of White labour, segregation provisions in the Factories Act and other legislation), minimum wage rates excluded Coloureds, Indians and Africans from the more productive and better-paid opportunities of employment. Moreover, the enforcement of the "rate for the job" destroyed the incentive for these races to improve their skills by their own efforts and savings, as well as the motive for entrepreneurial investment in their training. Indeed, if it had not been for the enforcement of the standard rate, I believe that most of the more obvious and direct exclusions of non-Whites from better-paid employment opportunities (which I am about to discuss) would have been *evaded* under the stimulus of the profit motive. The late Dr. Abdurahman, the greatest leader the Coloured people ever had, perceived this truth when, in the report of the Cape Coloured Commission of 1937, he declared:

Until equality of opportunity in the matter of education and technical training has been established, and until a greater measure of equality of consideration has been won, minimum wage legislation will generally work against the advancement of the Cape Coloured people. There is always a danger that enforced uniformity will react against the advantage of the least fortunate class.

The more open discriminations, even "job reservation," have been much less effective, in my opinion, in maintaining the subservience of the non-White classes than the enforcement of minimum wage rates. This has been because the races harmed have acquiesced. They have been indoctrinated into believing that their real enemy has been that fictitious abstraction, "the capitalist exploiter." [2]

(2) The Apprenticeship Act has also been used to enforce an effective colour bar. Well-meaning educationists who assisted in the drafting of this Act did not perceive that in practice it would work to prevent the indenturing of more than a negligible portion of non-Whites in the kinds of skilled work to which the Act applies.[3] Relatively few non-Whites have facilities for reaching the quite unnecessarily high minimum educational standards laid down, whilst the few who do achieve these standards tend, in any case, to be kept out by the "apprenticeship committees." These committees represent existing employees and employers, whilst the latter have usually been concerned more to maintain industrial harmony by appeasing their privileged White staff than to serve the interests of the community as consumers and provide openings for the underprivileged non-Whites. The "employers' representa-

[2] Actually, wage rates in South Africa have not been low in relation to the value of the product, in the low-productivity occupations to which standard rates have confined the majority. The lowest rates of wages are those of Africans. Yet they have been high enough to attract 800,000 foreign Africans from territories as far distant as Tanganyika.

[3] Thus, in the Cape, where there are an approximately equal number of Whites and Coloureds, less than a thousand Coloureds were indentured in 1960–1961 out of a total of more than thirteen thousand. Last century there had been more Coloured than White artisans.

tives" feel also that they may be penalized, through the many arbitrary powers which socialist legislation has conferred on the Government, if they fail to conform to what appears to be official policy.

(3) "Job reservation" which, *under that name,* has been introduced only recently (as an amendment of the Industrial Conciliation Act) forbids the performance of certain tasks by particular races. The colour bar in this case is quite blatant and open, although *the announced aim* is simply to protect the White man from "exploitation" by the other (poorer) races, and *to defend all, irrespective of race or colour,* from "interracial competition." How judicious such a claim is can be judged in the light of some actual reservations promulgated. In certain areas non-Whites may not serve as elevator attendants, drivers of specified vehicles, ambulance drivers (even when carrying non-Whites), traffic policemen (although they have been extremely successful in this role), firemen, barmen, masons, joiners, etc.

We can trace the origin of formal job reservation practices to the *Mines and Works Act* of 1911, which had the effect of keeping certain kinds of skilled work for Whites only in mining and associated activities. This Act, which became known as the first "Colour Bar Act," was intended to meet the demands of the White miners' labour unions, whose leaders, influenced by Marxist ideas and those of foreign leftist organizations like the Knights of Labour, the I.W.W. (anarchist) and French syndicalism, had organized strikes which were accompanied with violence and bloodshed. A strike in 1907, marked by sabotage and murder,[4] led to a labour-appeasing Transvaal Ordinance which protected Whites from competition from non-Whites. This

---

[4] Two members of the Miners' Association (the labour union) were charged with murder, but the evidence was inconclusive.

ordinance was the model and precedent for the two "Colour Bar Acts" of 1911 and 1926.[5]

In 1922 another violent strike was organized, in resistance to an attempt by the mining managements to secure some relaxation of the 1911 colour bar, so that certain kinds of semiskilled and skilled work could be performed by Africans. This strike was supported by a general strike on the I.W.W. model. The insurrection—for such it became—was crushed; but the impression had been created that "capitalist oppression" was threatening the privileges of the Whites and the traditional subordinacy of the Blacks. The result was that the South African Labour Party, a socialist party with a very similar outlook to that of the British Labour Party of the time, obtained office in 1924, through a coalition with the Nationalist (Calvinist and Afrikaner) Party. This party, also anti-capitalist in attitude,[6] was committed to the principle that there should be no equality in church or state between Black and White.

At once the "Pact Government," as the Labour–Nationalist coalition was called, introduced the "civilized labour policy," to which I have already referred, and passed the second great Colour Bar Act (the *Mines and Works Act* of 1926), which aimed at perpetuating the economic inferiority of the Africans. This Act enforced the most honest and unashamed colour discriminations which the world has ever known. It was a triumph for W. H.

5 There is an astonishing similarity between the form taken by the violent strikes in South Africa, which inspired the "Colour Bar Acts" of 1911 and 1926, and those which occurred about the same time, under I.W.W. incitement, in the United States.

6 My colleague, Professor H. M. Robertson has pointed to the "consciously anti-capitalistic" attitude of Afrikaner Calvinism. He quotes a recent Calvinistic pronouncement to the effect that "Socialism is a justified reaction against the abuses of Capitalism" (*Marx, Menger, Mercantilism and Max Weber*, in *Studi in Onore di Anitore Fanfani*, Vol. VI, 1962).

Andrews, who had played a major role not only in the 1922
strike but in several of the previous strikes which had involved violence. Almost immediately afterwards he became
Secretary of the Communist Party of South Africa.

(4) What is known as "Group Areas" legislation has also
imposed colour bars by preventing development in those
areas in which private entrepreneurial judgment would
have located productive activities. The immediate purpose
was the imposition by statute of a type of residental segregation which had often been arranged previously by private covenant or simple preference. Now if the Group Areas
policy had sought merely to maintain the *status quo,* it
would not have led to the burning resentments which it
has engendered. But when, under the socialist tradition,
the *power* to discriminate is accorded to the state, any
majority represented will almost inevitably demand discrimination against (or tolerate private discrimination
against) political minorities, or against the politically un-
represented, even although the latter may (as in South Africa) form the majority of the population.

This assertion is clearly illustrated in the Group Areas
administration. We find, for instance, that the more pleas-
ant residential districts of towns have been reserved for
the Whites, and the non-Whites have been ousted (after
due notice) when they have been living in such areas.
Moreover, the political power of a majority has been used,
almost sadistically, to impose *new and humiliating* segregations in public transport, in universities, in parks, libraries, theatres, sport, etc. Even learned societies have recently been called upon to exclude non-Whites if they (the
societies) wish to retain any government subsidy. (Most
learned societies will, I believe, prefer to forego the subsidy.) The *economic* injustices have been greatest when
businesses (including shops) owned by non-Whites have

been driven from areas in which they have for long served the relatively affluent White community. But the effect of the residential segregations has typically been to force the Coloureds, Indians and Africans to live further than before from their place of employment.

(5) More drastic than the Group Areas administration in the case of Africans has been "central economic planning," administered through what is known as "influx control." The Government and its agencies have been accorded powers of labour direction which are unparalleled outside the Iron Curtain countries. Under the Bantu Laws Amendment Bill, which is likely to become law next year, this more or less communistic pattern of control of African labour will be greatly intensified. The object is partly to force the Africans out of their existing urban industrial employments into what are known as "border industries" (that is, areas nearer to their original homelands) or into employment on the mines and the farms. It is all part of the territorial segregation aim of "separate development." This policy, which has created bitter resentment among urban Africans, is capable of being presented in a favorable light. But those who condemn it should begin by recognizing that such labour direction can be undertaken solely because socialistic or communistic powers have been accorded to governments. Under the unrestrained free market it could not happen.

(6) Not only has the "control" apparatus of socialism been used to keep the Africans, Coloureds and Indians in economic subordinacy, but direct and deliberate suppression of profit-activated initiatives has been resorted to for the same purpose. Thus, private investment from outside to develop the naturally poor African "reserves"—the areas of African ancestry—has been prohibited. Accordingly, when the Transkei (the land of origin of the Xhosa peo-

ple) was recently conceded a measure of local autonomy,[7]
a most vital right was excluded, namely, that of receiving
privately owned White capital as loans or investments. Any
Transkei industrial development requiring capital from
outside must obtain it from the state *via* the "Bantu Investment Corporation." Naturally, the plea has been that
these poor backward, ignorant Africans have to be protected from "exploitation"! "We will not let the wolves in
—those people who simply seek where they can make
money in order to fill their own pocket," said the Minister
of Bantu Administration. But in the opinion of some responsible critics, the real aim of this exclusion of capitalism has been to guarantee cheap labour for the farms and
the mines.

In the same spirit, Africans have recently been denied
the right to establish their own simple businesses (such as
shops, filling stations, garages, cinemas, etc.), even in their
urban "locations"—town districts specifically reserved for
their residence—and out of their own savings. Once again,
the claim has been that the purpose is to protect the Africans (as investors) from wasting their savings and (as consumers) from inferior services.

In the case of Indians, such social respect and status as
they have been able to command in my country has been
through their success in business, in which sphere they
have exercised enterprise, industry, business acumen and
thrift. The free market and scope for profit-seeking have
allowed them to progress in spite of powerful race prejudice. Is it surprising that, in the hope of maintaining the
Indians permanently in their present inferiority of social
position and material condition, it should have been

7 This move has been publicized abroad as "self-government," but the
constitution of the Transkei seems to ensure the dominance of the chiefs
and the unprogressive tribal system. It requires all measures passed by the
Transkei Legislative Assembly to be submitted for the approval of the Republic Government.

thought essential to curtail these channels of advancement through land tenure and group areas legislation? The method has been simply to remove their contact with the most profitable markets, which are situated in White shopping areas.

(7) In the public service the maintenance of colour bars has been easiest. Unlike the free market, the state is seldom colour-blind. Hence the nationalization of certain industries has been an effective method of restraining the tendency of private enterprise to permit the poorer races *to contribute a greater value to and draw a greater value from* the common pool. The opportunities for non-Whites in state employments have been confined almost entirely to "put and carry work," and even then only when no Whites have been available for it. In times of depression, the replacement of non-Whites by Whites in unskilled work has been regarded as a defensible way of providing relief; and the Minister of Railways recently admitted that more than 10,000 White railwaymen (he could have said "voters") were employed in order to prevent them from becoming a burden on the community. In fact, this featherbedding has removed the incentive for these easy-going people (of the "poor White" type) to adjust themselves more effectively to the contemporary economic world.

It may well be objected that the "capitalists"—investors and business managements—must accept at least part of the blame for apartheid because they have, after all, acquiesced in the system. I do not suggest that they have not often shared the colour attitudes which have led to the erection or maintenance of colour bars. Yet I have shown that such barriers are contrary to the interests of the whole commercial and industrial world; and the businessman's colour prejudices begin to dissolve when they affect his pocket adversely. The opposition of business leaders has been less

effective than it could have been because many have been
intimidated. The ability of state servants and agencies to
create or destroy private fortunes has inhibited open and
potent political opposition. Socialistic powers necessarily
create fears that official discretion may quietly discriminate
against those who actively oppose or criticize governments.
The result has been a deplorable obsequiousness towards
ministers and top officials. It is this, added to the desire of
managements to maintain staff harmony by the appease-
ment of White employees, which has limited the effectiveness of the profit motive. But this motive has, nevertheless,
remained the most powerful force tending throughout to
uplift the underprivileged races.

We see, then, that the restraints on equality of opportunity as between the different races in South Africa are
all of a kind which are applauded in leftist circles everywhere. Yet *the parties of the left* (even in South Africa
itself) *have been loudest in their condemnation of the traditional segregation (now called "apartheid") for the survival of which their own ideologies have been mainly
responsible!* The leftists have conspicuously and universally defended or advocated "the rate for the job" as a
principle in labour remuneration; and as we have seen,
*it is this principle which has created the most insidious and
vicious of all colour bars.*

Of course, by reason of the dogmatic convictions which
actuate them, the socialists must oppose the profit-seeking
(loss-avoidance) incentives. This may in part explain why
the form of leftist opposition to apartheid seems so often to
have been designed to aggravate rather than mitigate that
system. Frequently the apparent aim has been to *exacer-
bate* the understandable fears of the privileged races. The
precipitation of political disorder by the temporary perpetuation of racial injustices may have been judged to be
the most effective method of promoting the "liberation"

of the non-Whites *via* violence and revolution. But I cannot help thinking that pro-Soviet propagandists everywhere have recognized only too realistically that apartheid has provided them with the ideal platform in their campaign to encourage Black imperialism.

I have sympathy with those Black leaders who regard the racial policies of my country as a lamentable affront to the dignity of the non-White races. I am not surprised, indeed, that many articulate Africans have developed a fanatical and undiscriminating hatred of our Whites. But they ought to view our policies objectively and in their historical setting. Our politicians have been trying, however ineptly, to find a solution to problems of enormous complexity. The apartheid program of 1949 was the first groping step taken to deal with an explosive issue which the politicians had been trying to avoid for half a century. It was chosen because it seemed to be the most acceptable move politically, given the stereotypes of the White electorate. The easy way to office was to pander to race prejudice and the desire for continued "baasskap" (domination by the Whites). But in their hearts all the politicians now know that the move to preserve "baasskap" was a false step; and in spite of unashamed indoctrination (through broadcasting, the Afrikaans press and an English language weekly), there never has been a period in which colour attitudes have been subject to such rapid readjustment as in South Africa today. In my opinion apartheid, even if softened by successive modifications, will prove to have been an ephemeral episode, a mere stage in the rapidly changing relations between races.[8] We are begin-

[8] I cannot here deal with the proposals to prepare the Africans for ultimate self-government in their traditional "reserves." If this were sincerely meant and involved the early inclusion in the self-governed areas of (a) the "border industrial areas," (b) a large proportion of the agricultural land of the Free State and the Transvaal and (c) at least one major port (Port Elizabeth is the obvious choice), that could make the "Bantustans,"

ning to hear talk of "liberal Nationalists," and it is significant that our Minister of Defense recently used the phrase,
"world opinion cannot be fought." The Government's
difficulty is, in the words of the *Cape Argus*, that it is "in
power by virtue of support from a party which does not,
at the rank and file level, agree with any basic change in
what originally it was told apartheid meant."

The major obstacle to an early relinquishment of racial
discrimination is that created by the insistence upon "one
man, one vote" by most of the Government's critics. For
any extension of the franchise which does not embody, in
ironclad constitutional entrenchments, some principle of
weighting to protect the rights and property of the
Whites, the Coloureds and the Indians, or which does not,
alternatively, incorporate the Tocqueville principle that
majorities may not enrich themselves at the expense of the
minorities, would rapidly lead to chaos. Without such safe-
guards, the universal franchise would simply replace the
present system in which a minority exploits the majority
by a system in which a majority would exploit minorities.

The existing complex of colour attitudes has this to be
said in its defense, that it evolved over the course of history
with the *active approval* of the Dutch Reformed churches
and, until recently, with the *acquiescence*—however uneasy—of the other churches in South Africa. What *has* become indefensible is *the attempted perpetuation* of the
situation by legislation; but the mere replacement of the
present regime, which involves the protection of *historically determined injustices* towards the non-Whites, by
deliberately created injustices towards the Whites is even
less defensible; and that is what irresponsible critics of my

---

as the projected areas are known, viable. Some people (hardly realistically,
I feel) think that some such partition is the secret aim of the present Government, although it would be politically fatal at this stage for them to dis-
close this objective to their supporters.

country are demanding. After all, the Whites have been the architects of civilized South Africa; and those who would suffer most under political domination by the Africans, are persons, classes and races who have been least responsible for the maintenance of the barriers to African achievement. The Coloured people and the Indians have, in my opinion, been even more viciously treated under apartheid than the Africans.[9] But they too would need constitutional protection of their rights and property under any extension of the franchise.

In the shrewd conduct of the Cold War, the Communists have been using the Afro-Asian Bloc and the United Nations to play on the perfectly natural resentment of the Black or non-White races at surviving White arrogance and White privileges. It almost seems as if it has been their aim to prevent at all costs a bloodless abandonment of colour injustices. They have sought to provoke sheer envy and the desire for vengeance. Yet the United Nations and Britain, in their laudable object of winning the goodwill of the African states, *appear* to have given almost reckless moral support to the Black nationalism and Black imperialism inspired by these passions.

Certainly fears of the future—even threats from abroad—may have been needed to force us to an agonizing reappraisal of issues on which we have all too long inhibited thought. Insofar as the foreign critics of my country are succeeding (through the United Nations, through diplomatic representation, or through the press) in disturbing our surviving beliefs that we can, for an indefinite period, exclude effective competition from the non-Whites (which means denying them equal opportunities), they are rendering all of us an invaluable service. But insofar as our critics seem to be urging us to accept a situation in which a minority of Whites (who at present monopolize political

9 They have suffered most from deliberately inflicted humiliations.

power) must share parliamentary representation with a formerly disenfranchised group three times as large, without rigid constitutional entrenchments to protect the minorities from spoliation and revenge, they are prolonging the era against which they fulminate. For apprehension of the disaster which any unconditional universal franchise must threaten in South Africa is the chief discouragement of that readjustment of ideas among the Whites which can alone make possible, without a devastating and bloody revolution, the gradual and orderly elimination of colour bars.

Our thinking is more likely to be constructive if the Western powers recognize our dilemma and make clear their determination to assist those of us who wish to defend, not the *privileges* of the Whites (or the right of any race to show contempt for another), but the right of the Whites to *entrenched protection as a minority*. Our critics from abroad must perceive the reasonableness of our insistence upon some defense against avarice and vindictiveness. For are not these vices to be expected from newly enfranchised peoples with a tribal background? [10] Pressures from abroad would have an incomparably greater influence if they explicitly recognized this issue.

To prove our sincerity we could certainly be expected to agree to the generalization, for the benefit of all the non-White races, of the constitutional protections which we Whites must surely demand. In other words, we may appropriately be called upon to accept the entrenchment also of the principle of non-discrimination.[11] Such an entrench-

[10] I must not be misunderstood on this point. *Tribal* Africans certainly do not show vindictiveness or avarice. What I fear is that politicians seeking votes will create these vices. Whites, Africans and Coloureds have long lived on terms of amity in the reserves. Indeed, the traditional racial goodwill has been remarkable.

[11] The great exposition of this principle is in Hayek's *Constitution of Liberty*.

ment would accord to independent courts (after a defined period of adjustment—*also entrenched*) the duty to declare unconstitutional all legislation, ordinances or bylaws which discriminate, directly or indirectly, in favor of particular races, particular sexes, particular social classes, particular income groups, or particular professions and occupations. And because such discriminations might be imposed, not by the state itself, but (by reason of state acquiescence) through the private use of coercive power in forms such as boycotts, lock-outs, strikes and similar practices, we could be expected to agree also to entrenched provisions which render void and unenforceable all collective agreements and contracts which, directly or indirectly, have the effect of imposing discriminations. In particular, if there is any class or race against the employment of which, in any sphere, there is a barrier of prejudice, custom or historical circumstance, that class or race must have the *constitutional* right to discount its initial inferiority in the employment field.

I cannot here deal with the difficulties which would be involved in any *peaceful transition* to such a non-discriminatory regime. But I can point to its inherent feasibility; the most important effect of the gradual establishment of equality of opportunity would be an enormous increase in the community's real income, through the more efficient use and development of labour resources; and this would provide a fund for compensation of that minority of formerly privileged *individuals* (not of races or classes) whose established expectations were catastrophically upset. By such a stratagem it should be possible to dissolve privilege peacefully and rapidly in the course of one generation.

But whether we can expect encouragement for a non-violent solution from countries like the United States and Britain is, unfortunately, very doubtful. For the electorates of these countries have been indoctrinated with the notion that democracy means what Mises has called "omnipotent government" and that economic justice implies the impartial granting of favours and welfare to all by a benevolent state. When government is regarded, not as a neutral instrument but as a bountiful donor of benefits whom the people must propitiate, "political might is social right" becomes enshrined as the supreme ethical principle.

9   The Bantustans

PAUL GINIEWSKI

PAUL GINIEWSKI, *editor-in-chief of* La Terre Retrouvée *in Paris, is a free-lance correspondent for many European newspapers and magazines, including* Politique Etrangère, Revue de Psychologie des Peuples, La Suisse, Tribune de Lausanne, Europa Archiv, Revista di Studi Politici Internazionali.
  Among his books are Israel devant L'Afrique et L'Asie *(1958) and* Bantustans: A Trek Towards the Future *(1961).*

The years 1963–64 which saw the collapse of the Federation of Nyasaland and the Rhodesias and the start of revolutionary activity in Angola will have seen the end of an important stage, probably the final step, in the process of decolonization which started in Africa after the Second World War. This process was a sort of top to bottom raising of a curtain: the curtain was lifted freeing the continent, starting from the north and ending in the south, with the single notable exception of Algeria. This phenomenon of decolonization has now reached the southern tip of the continent and to believe that that part of Africa can indefinitely hold aloof from an irreversible historic develop-

175

ment is altogether unreasonable. The best we can hope for, what it is the duty of statesmen and of international institutions to work towards, is to find a form of decolonization suitable for South Africa on the basis of the experiences and insights gained in the past decade and a half. A solution for South Africa must be found which will take into account its very unique character in Africa.

South Africa is not a "colony," where a group of colonists is superimposed on a native population, but a country in which distinct and legitimate national groups coexist. And one of these national groups, in sharp contrast to other colonial situations, has no country where it can live in exile or to which it can return after independence (*i.e.*, the Dutch in Indonesia returned to the Netherlands, the British in Kenya to England, the French in Algeria to France). Former Prime Minister Macmillan once said, with reason, that "the nationalism of the whites of South Africa is the first in point of time of the African nationalisms." The white South Africans have as legitimate a claim to the territory they occupy as the Ghanaians or the Congolese do to theirs. Did not the first Dutch colonists debark at the Cape around 1652 (the same year other Dutchmen founded New York) and settle the country from south to north, at the very moment the Bantus were crossing the Limpopo River to the north, and moving southward?

The debate in the United Nations now is over the question of apartheid and over South Africa's mandate over South-West Africa. It is clear, at the outset, that what South Africa faces is a problem infinitely more complex than that of a colonial society engaged in a rearguard action, or of a government practicing racial discrimination against a colored population. What we have here is an industrialized, developed *African* state (we should not forget that "Afrikaner" means, simply, African) with underdeveloped, nonindustrialized "colonies," also African, in the

heart of its own territory. What must be worked out is a
totally new method of decolonization. It is a hard problem.
If the United Nations, in the crucial years ahead, musters
the wisdom to work out a compromise that will safeguard
the rights of both legitimate national groups of South
Africa, the Bantus and the Whites, it will not be a political
victory of one ideology over another, of one "race" over
another, it will be a major contribution to Africa.

David Ben-Gurion has truthfully observed that "the
Cold War between East and West is above all the battle for
the souls and the minds of the peoples of Africa and Asia."
This battle is being fought first and foremost in the debating halls of the United Nations. There, it is far easier for
the ideologues to make their points and stage their spectacular victories: in the jungles the unpublicized devotion of
technicians, doctors and teachers produces no political fire-
works. The question is: Will the United Nations act
positively, with wisdom and justice, in the matter of the
decolonization of South Africa? In other words, will it find
a solution which deserves support and applause because of
its real merit, or will it settle instead for pompous formu-
lations with no intrinsic merit.

What course of action might the United Nations suggest
for South Africa?

It is clearly morally right to work for an end to the
apartheid policy. I am unreservedly in favor of suppression
of all racial discrimination. But apartheid is a *negative*
phenomenon: a passing and unpleasant phenomenon, but
not in the long-term scheme of things a focal point for concentrating effort. It is the positive problem of the political
impotence of the Negro in South Africa which seems to me
to demand a solution, and in my opinion, given the present
political climate in Africa, it can only be accomplished, as
in Ghana or the Congo, by national independence. The
eleven and a half million Bantus of South Africa must be

given a state, but not at the expense of destroying the
White state or of so altering both as to deprive Africa of
one of its major assets. This can not be done, in my opinion, except through partition. Many apparently intractable
problems of conflicting groups within the same political
boundaries have been solved by partition. India, Palestine,
Ireland, are examples. Even the marvelous unity of the
Scandinavian nations is the result of a partition; these
countries fought furiously among themselves until they
were split into different political units. To expel South
Africa from the United Nations or to apply sanctions and
boycotts would be to attack a sympton, not a cause. We
should rather attack the cause which produces the effect.
But how?

II

Actually South Africa has taken a path toward independence for the Bantus by her policy of "separate development," the positive counterpart of apartheid. And this
policy is further advanced and more irreversible than is
generally supposed. Countries in the United Nations
which now oppose this separate development should, instead, throw all their support to it in order to ensure its
successful conclusion. What does it consist of?

Political Aspects of the Problem

As the anti-South Africa offensive gathers steam around
the world, a political experiment is taking place in the
Transkei which could change the situation from top to
bottom. The Transkei, in truth, is more than an experiment. In a territory in which one and a half million Negroes live, an embryonic independent state is being formed
that could, if this experiment is carried through, lead to

the partition of South Africa into a residual white state and a new black state.

Early in 1963, the South African parliament voted a constitution for the Transkei. This constitution set up, first of all, symbols: a flag for the Transkei (which will, at first, be flown side by side with the flag of the Republic); a national anthem (whose title is, significantly, "May the Lord bless Africa"); a citizenship in the Transkei. In the present climate in Africa simply putting these symbols into effect has its impact. (Theodore Herzl, the organizer of the Zionist movement that brought into being the State of Israel, once made the acute remark that a flag is nothing but a piece of cloth nailed to a stick, but that with a flag men can be led anywhere.) But the constitution went much further. It also founded institutions: a legislative assembly composed of the sixty-four tribal Supreme Chiefs of the Transkei and forty-five deputies elected by universal suffrage; six ministries (justice, education, finance, transport, interior, social affairs), removed from the jurisdiction of the white government in Pretoria and placed under Bantu ministers at Umtata, the capital of the territory; a Prime Minister. On November 20, 1963, the electors chose their forty-five deputies. A little later, Chief Kaiser Matanzima was nominated as Prime Minister by the assembly.

The elections in the Transkei and the setting up of a Bantu government which will control only matters of secondary importance (defense, foreign affairs, etc., will remain in the hands of the white government in Pretoria) might seem, *a priori,* a totally inadequate solution to the political impotence of the blacks in South Africa. It is clear that if the steps were to stop here, it would be nothing but a palliative, totally invalid and in any case without effect on the Negroes in the big cities and the rural inhabitants of the other "reservations." But we should look at the initiatives taken in the Transkei as first steps, as an example of what should be done as rapidly as possible in the other less-developed reservations. Chief Kaiser Mantan-zima, who represents the more moderate tendencies in the Transkei, does not conceal his intention of enlarging the internal autonomy granted the Transkei by the constitution, in successive steps, to the point where the problem of independence will have to be faced. (In point of fact, the constitution provides for the ultimate transfer of other ministries to the Transkei.) Mantanzima, regarded on one side by his political opponents as a quisling, has also made demands which the other side regards as extreme, notably, his insistence that Whites now living in the Transkei be ousted and that certain lands be included in his territory that the government seems to have no intention of relinquishing.

The whole move worries certain white circles who refuse to take the Bantustans seriously and regard them only as a smokescreen behind which the cruel realities of apartheid can be masked. But it has also reassured those Whites (they are at present a minority) who are prepared to make whatever moral, financial and territorial sacrifices prove necessary to pursue the Bantustan policy to its necessary conclusion. "Once you start to organize elections you might just as well reconcile yourself to surrender," a South African leader said recently. And, in the historic perspective, this is correct. It is with this perspective in mind that one must judge the Transkei experiment.

Therefore, the Transkei experiment might prove a race against the clock between white South Africa and the black nationalist movements and their natural allies in Africa and the United Nations: Will the Transkei lead the way, by gradual steps, toward an independent Negro state in a partitioned South Africa, or will apartheid be continued and another Algerian war result?

Who will first attain his objectives? The Whites who

sincerely hope to liquidate apartheid by careful surgery? Or the extremists among the Negroes, who want a hot-headed solution and who would like, at the very least, to be at the same point as the revolutionaries in Angola? Which will first understand that to win out he must act more speedily and with greater initiative than his opponent? Will either side understand that it is to the interest of the world at large that a peaceful solution be found for this problem: in the interest of the three million Whites who have no other homes; in the interest of the Bantus of South Africa who have a right, as have their brother Africans, not only to social emancipation but to national independence; in the interest, finally, of Africa in which an industrialized and highly developed South Africa should play an important role?

The Utopian Aspects of the Problem

Opponents of the Bantustans say the concept is utopian. But history is a fabric of utopias that have become realities. A comparison with a recent political utopia, the Zionist ideal that resulted in the Jewish state, seems appropriate. Let us examine that story for the useful parallels it holds with the Bantu situation.

It was in 1897 that Theodore Herzl wrote *The Jewish State*. The book and the idea were then, in the eyes of political men and in the eyes of the Jewish intelligentsia, utopian. Far more utopian than the utopia of the Bantustans. Only the Jews of Russia, those disinherited masses living in ghettos ("reservations") from which they were forbidden to move under a system of segregated ethnic groups very similar to the "Group Areas Act" of South Africa, took it seriously. These Jews carried a special passport, as do the Bantus of South Africa. To them, a territorial solution in Palestine, such as Herzl outlined, seemed the answer to all their sufferings under a Czarist-apartheid.

Today, the educated Bantu intelligentsia rejects the Bantustan solution and looks instead to social and political integration with the Whites. But it is a losing proposition, because this integration cannot be achieved along the American model where the proportion of Negroes to Whites and the cultural level of the Negro are totally different. I believe this elite will rejoin the masses when utopia becomes reality; when the Bantustans are able to provide them with jobs, honors and posts of authority.

The Zionist utopia took a long time in coming, a long time to convince the incredulous. British authorities in Palestine did their best to brake the movement by imposing on it the restrictive "capacity of absorption" policy, based on the capacity of the country to receive immigrants, the capacity of industry and commerce to absorb new capital. One commission of inquiry after another concluded that there was no more capacity for absorption in the country. These same conclusions are being reached *a priori* about the Transkei. Far from being able to house all the Xhosas of South Africa, the Transkei will not even be able to support those Xhosas who already live on its overpopulated soil, so say the opponents of the Bantustans. It is true that the partisans of the Bantustan policy (such is their irresolution!) encourage this position by their insistence that self-government, progress and civilization can only be introduced at a very slow pace in an Africa which is still, today, the Africa of the oxcart and canoe. To hold such pessimistic views is worse than a crime: a mistake. . . .

Of course, certain aspects of African life cannot be accelerated, but others, which would remain static if left alone, can be; and it is in pressing forward here and there, wherever possible, that a solution lies. It is because the South African Government has not yet discovered which processes to push and which to allow to mature at their own pace, that its static Bantu policy deserves criticism. And here again a comparison with Zionism is instructive.

In the heroic days of Zionism, there were also militants who demanded a faster tempo, the attainment of political power before the economic realities had been dealt with. But the present leaders of Israel, David Ben-Gurion among them, always favored a slow but sure, stage-by-stage development. They were called traitors and quislings by their impatient adversaries within the Zionist camp for collaborating with the British Government, as the partisans of the Bantu states today are being called traitors and quislings. Indeed, a majority of Jews opposed the very idea of a Jewish state; the majority of Jews dreamed of staying in their own lands and being fully integrated with their countrymen, of being Jews to be sure, but "German Jews," "French Jews," etc. The Zionists were a tiny minority.

Since then, utopia has become reality. Zionism and integration coexist, but historically, it is the Zionists who have won the battle among the Jews. The "German Jews," the "French Jews" can survive as individuals (and everyone knows what a tiny percentage of them survived the Nazi holocaust), but historically it is the Israeli Jews who will perpetuate the Jewish race. This parallel throws light on the Bantu situation. The Jews had dreamed of entrusting their safety and peace to moral progress in an increasingly democratic world. The Bantus dream that too. The Jews of Europe lost six million of their people, atrociously assassinated, through having put their faith in democracy and moral progress. The lesson is clear: only when the secular state acts to protect its own citizens does it, incidentally, protect mankind. Will the Bantus understand this lesson? Will the "winds of change" that are sweeping Africa, and the pressures from snowballing independent regimes that look toward South Africa with anger, have an unexpected result and end by crystallizing a Bantu

Zionism that will demand redress for the discriminations of apartheid in the name of, and through, a Bantu state? Did not the Jews who chose Israel put an end to persecutions by becoming their own masters? They forestalled a Nasser pogrom in 1956, as they will any time it proves necessary, by going to war.

The Moral Aspect of the Problem

In my book *Bantustans*,[1] I expressed the same fundamental doubt that all foreign observers feel about South Africa, namely: to what degree is its "separate development" policy (whose ultimate aim, said the Prime Minister in 1959, is to make the Bantus as free as the Ghanaians are today) a serious undertaking? In the course of my investigation and in line with my doubts, I even considered entitling my book: *Anatomy of a Smokescreen,* which would have been self-explanatory. I decided finally against this title. I believe that we must not only firmly and optimistically hope that this policy will succeed, we must see to it that it does succeed. Not only should the United Nations assume responsibility for (and take at its face value) the policy of separate development, the people of South Africa as a whole should bring pressure on their government to accelerate the development of the Bantustans. The vote is not the only instrument that can be used in a democracy to express approbation or disapprobation. A gamut of other popular pressures can be applied, both peacefully and legally.

What are the methods? They are legion. A few examples should suffice to indicate the kind of thing I mean.

White boy scouts in South Africa (and particularly the

---

1 English edition: *Bantustans, A Trek Towards the Future* (Cape Town: Human & Rousseau, 1961). French edition: *Une Autre Afrique du Sud* (Paris: Editions Berger-Levrault, 1962).

Voortrekkers, the Afrikaner scouts) could organize jam-
borees and camps in the Transkei. I have noticed how few
people in South Africa know the Transkei. Would the
Bantu authorities in Umtata and the government in Pretoria oppose (and if they did, would they not unmask their
own hypocrisy) a popular movement to instruct the Transkei youth in scouting? A national collection could be
launched to finance investments in the Transkei, in which
every South African could participate. Did not the Zionists buy back the soil of Palestine, cent by cent, *pfennig* by
pfennig, penny by penny, with the blue and white box of
the Jewish National Fund which was placed in hundreds
of thousands of Jewish households throughout the world?
White cities and towns could enter into twin city programs
with Bantu villages.

In sum, one would like to see a great national upsurge
to aid both the physical and spiritual construction of the
Bantustans. The white man, as Kipling once said, has assumed a heavy burden in Africa. That is more true today
than ever. One would like to see youth movements calling
on their members to give up a week or a month to laboring
in the workshops of Umtata or in Pondoland; to see
women's groups launch campaigns to help feed under-
nourished Bantu infants. Could there not be a slight raise
in postal rates that would be used to finance construction
of schools in the reservations? There are hundreds of programs that could be initiated; they are not charity (charity
can do nothing to solve the national problems of the
Bantus). They would be signs of an immense outpouring
of conscience, of a spiritual investment, of an enthusiasm
for the bringing into being of the Bantustans. (I confess I
have not yet encountered such a spirit.) But could not a
spectacular movement of this sort have as great an effect as
the political initiatives the Government has taken?

In the individual and voluntary mobilizing of popular

opinion for a political idea, government policy can be transformed into the endeavor of the whole nation. The policy of separate development should be imbued with the "milk of human kindness" to make it, as it is in theory, a method of elevating instead of debasing the Bantus. A South African organization, The South Africa Foundation, has created a slogan "man to man" for its program of explaining to foreigners "man to man" the difficult South African situation. Psychologically the idea is right. But if there is good reason to build bridges between South Africa and the rest of the world, between Johannesburg and New York, is there not even better reason to build bridges within the country, between Johannesburg and Umtata?

If South Africa grasped this problem of decolonization in the same resolute fashion in which it would fight a war, it could dispel the confusion which prevails concerning its policies; it now seems to most people that one has to be automatically (a) against apartheid and against the Bantustans, or (b) for apartheid and for the Bantustans, with the inference being that the pro-Bantustan forces are "fascists" and their opponents "democrats."

This dichotomy has a parallel in Bantu thinking (perhaps it finds its roots there), where the choice, seemingly, is limited to becoming a "white" black and abandoning one's negritude, or remaining a Bantu and conserving one's backward past. The choice would be between total negritude and whiteness, with the stigmata of the one and the quality of the other automatically and forever attached to the color of the skin. Nothing is more absurdly racist and false; and this double racism, of the Negro and the White, has led the Negroes and Whites of South Africa to nothing but a series of impasses.

The simplistic choice between White and civilized and Bantu and backward must be relegated to the storehouse of outdated colonial accessories. Personally, I am opposed to all the discriminatory laws of apartheid. But it is for that very reason that I am a partisan of the Bantu states, and it's just too bad if this position does not coincide with the too-easy slogans of the anti-colonial propagandists or with the archaic notions of those who insist upon the *status quo*. After the bitter lesson of Nazi Germany, no one should believe that a degree of civilization is linked automatically to the whiteness of skin. It would be easier to conclude the opposite. I believe that the Bantu must attain, and with all of us together surpass, that degree of civilization which the white race had attained before Germany sullied it, and that in attaining this the Bantus can remain faithful to their culture and their past.

There are no hierarchies in cultures. The Negro race is capable of all the levels and all the nuances of the European cultures, of all their values and technical abilities, just as the Afrikaner way of life, the American way of life, the Israeli "haloutsiouth" etc., are capable, each in their own manner and style, of producing their Moses, their Einstein, their Glenn.

Historic Perspective of the Bantustan Policy

The historic perspective of the separate development policy of the Bantus of South Africa carried to its logical end, independence, cannot be judged solely by that policy; it must also be seen in the context of the Africa in which it was developed. The lessons learned in recent years demonstrate that when insufficient and inadequate preparations have been made for independence, the nations thus liberated may find themselves facing political, economic and social situations which are little or no better than their condition as colonies.

Time magazine (July 6, 1962) gave a brief but striking account of the situation in the former Belgian Congo, under the melancholy headline, "After Two Years":

The new nation lies exhausted in the equatorial sun, a battered giant unable to make productive use of the freedom its black leaders fought so hard to win. Even with the help of nearly 3,000 Belgian and UN technicians and advisers and $86 million of U.S. financial aid, the railroads are not running in most of the Congo, two-thirds of the nation's trucks are idle for lack of spare parts, and the roads are almost impassable.

Coffee and cotton exports yielded only fractions of their normal revenue, and much of the big palm-oil output is lost to smugglers. Unemployed workers up country now flock to Léopoldville where 100,000 of the normal 300,000 labor force are already out of work. Organized gangs steal what they can.

Except for locally made beer and cigarettes, Léo's shops are virtually empty of consumer goods, and prices for the items still available have soared. No end to inflation is in sight, since Adoula's central government simply prints more and more money to make up for its hideous deficits.

The nightmarish political mess forces Adoula to spend 80% of his budget on salaries for civil servants and the 25,000-man army, which is vastly overpaid ($180 base pay per month for privates) to keep it loyal. To retain the support of the myriad political factions, he has 41 men in his cabinet, perhaps the world's biggest.

Corruption is widespread among the highest-ranking officials. There is a huge smuggling trade in diamonds. . . . Of some 17 million carats produced in South Kasai during the past year, only about 124,000 carats came onto the market legally.

An even blacker picture (no play on words) is given by René Dumont in his book *Black Africa Gets a Bad Start* (*L'Afrique Noire est mal partie*) which was reviewed in these striking terms by *l'Express,* one of the most anticolonialist French magazines, which has played an important part in the intellectual agitation for the liberation of enslaved peoples. In its issue of August 23, 1962, reviewing the Dumont book, *Express* asks: "Is this the soured judgment of an advocate of colonial Africa?" "Absolutely not," it answers. "René Dumont is a strong advocate of decolonization." René Dumont's report, more subtle than that in *Time*, is even more disturbing. I quote from *l'Express:*

> Gabon has one deputy for each 6,000 inhabitants, as against 100,000 in France. . . . [The government] has at its command a tremendous and overpaid civil service. The administrative expenses, which are not productive, absorb, for example, 60% of the internal budgetary receipts of Dahomey. Such a situation "is leading the African states to ruin."
>
> President Fulbert Youlou * wants to build himself a little Versailles and he is going to hire a Swiss to build it for him. President Houphouët-Boigny dresses in French livery the footmen and servitors of his palace, which coss nearly four billion [francs]. (Hundreds of tons of marble are believed to have been imported from Italy by air.) In the residential sections, bureaucrats live in superb villas and whiskey flows freely. For too many of the African elite, independence has consisted in taking the place of the whites and in enjoying the exorbitant advantages which the colonists had enjoyed.
>
> Family ties, ethnic bonds, nepotism all contribute to the parceling out of sinecures and good jobs in the capitals. . . . Finally, the sudden accession to power has disturbed certain individuals and corrupted their moral sense. Since independence, corruption has reached frightening proportions in Central Africa, in the Congo, in Dahomey, in the Ivory Coast, in the Cameroons. . . .
>
> In a word [I repeat, I am here quoting from a stoutly anticolonial journal] the sovereignty of the African states has created a privileged and overpaid class. A deputy works about

---

* Ousted in August, 1963, and accused of heading a "corrupt" government.

three months a year and earns nearly 3,000 francs a month.
That is more than in Greece or in Portugal. But more important, each month's salary represents what the average African
peasant earns in six years of work!

Such a situation, says René Dumont, is especially dangerous.
It is the fruit of our subsidies which permit these African governments to make both ends meet without having had to face
up to the real difficulties. There has been a flight from responsibilities instead of assumption of austerity measures or of getting to work. The result is that black Africa is moving toward
a sort of "South Americanization." Breweries and Coca-Cola
factories are going up in Abidjan, but for René Dumont the
Treichville quarter with its shantytowns and jerry-built houses
brings to mind the shacks of Rio de Janeiro. . . .

At the same time, the African peasant feels that he is being
pushed down, not to say despised. His lot has not changed at
all, but face to face with the Mercedes of these gentlemen of
Yaounde or the Chevrolet of the bureaucrats of Abidjan, he
takes on the mental attitude of a proletarian, of one exploited. . . .

Can one talk of democracy when certain dictatorships
are but lightly disguised, asks René Dumont? Hardly any
opposition, even a constructive opposition, has an opportunity to be heard. "The decolonization which is the most
urgent," he writes, "is of the people from the majority of
their African leaders." He recounts that in the Cameroons
one Negro recently was applauded when he stated: "Recolonization, that is to say the transfer of power to the
Whites, would be adopted by a crushing majority were
there a referendum on the question of 'continued independence or recolonization.'" It seems incredible!

No doubt, such criticisms sit badly with those African
leaders who refuse to allow any constructive opposition to
exist. But these findings should be examined by the real
statesmen among the African leaders, of whom there are a
number. An enumeration of the errors and faults of the

present regimes would serve no constructive purpose unless it tended to isolate the causes of the problems in order
to work out suitable remedies.

K. M. Panikkar, the Indian diplomat, whose credentials
as an anti-colonialist and as a devoted champion of the underdeveloped peoples are above reproach, has also commented on the lack of preparation for independence of the
new African states in his book, *The Afro-Asian States
and Their Problems:*

> Each one of these States during the last ten years has at-
> tempted to work a representative form of government with
> cabinets, parliaments and other paraphernalia of democracy.
> And yet it is clear that in most cases the full implications of
> this system of government have not been understood, not only
> by the people but by the leaders themselves. Their previous
> experience has not been generally related to democratic meth-
> ods of government or administration. In most cases the psy-
> chological background necessary for a government by the
> people was also absent.[2]

And Panikkar goes on to dig out the causes of the pseudo-
democracy that obtains in certain of the new states.

> The new States have in the main copied their institutions
> from the metropolitan power which ruled them without mak-
> ing any effort to distinguish between what is essential and what
> is incidental. They have, in fact, become text book democra-
> cies, with but little relation, in most cases, to the social and
> economic conditions of the countries concerned. The conse-
> quence is that in many of them there is an air of unreality—an
> attitude of make-believe.[3]

I would like to emphasize that in concluding my remarks
on the decolonization of South Africa with these bitter

[2] London: George Allen and Unwin Ltd., New York: The John Day Co.,
1959, p. 17.
[3] *Ibid.,* p. 25.

citations I do not seek to justify, because of the errors committed in certain new states, the unjustifiable aspects of the South African policy, notably the discrimination laws; I think they must be repealed unconditionally and without delay to purify the atmosphere and to allow the building of a new structure. I have cited the remarks of René Dumont and of K. M. Panikkar to show what in the universal and undiscriminating thirst for emancipation is conducive and what inimical to the social health of the people to be emancipated, to demonstrate that the accelerating tremors of independence have only too often been treated with the kind of radical nostrums that assuage by killing the patient or crippling him for life.

South Africa, which has a heavy responsibility for decolonizing its own territory, differs from the classical colonial powers in that the white South Africans are themselves part of the indigenous population. As I have said before (it cannot be said too often), it is not by accident that the colonists of Dutch descent, who arrived in the country at the same time as the Bantus, called themselves "Afrikaners." The spirit of *their* nationalism blows as strongly as does the nationalistic feelings of the Negroes in Africa. But these descendants of colonists, who have been living on their soil for so long that they are no longer colonists, refuse to promote a chaotic kind of independence; they cannot, as other colonists, return to their nations of origin, and wash their hands of their erstwhile colony. Perhaps the better among the white South Africans are trying unconsciously to establish a relationship between White and Bantu which reminds one of Valery's profound observations on friendship. Misunderstandings, he said, so often occur when people, not realizing that there is something precious in the fundamental differences that divide them, try to suppress these differences instead of making them the key for accord. How many of the noblest enterprises have foundered on the impossible and disastrous attempt to level out fundamental differences! How difficult it is, but how worthwhile, to find the key for such an accord! Many Negroes know this as well as Whites, and they have favored adopting the key of a common harmony whose music, once the Bantustans are in existence, will add a note of peace to that UN "concert of nations" which today produces more wailings than harmonies.

I remember the coming of age of Homolise, a young South African chief, at which his father made a most pertinent speech to an assembly which probably understood only a part of it. "The black man and the white man in South Africa are like two hands of a human being," he said. "They are joined to the same body. One is the left hand, one the right. For me, the white is the right hand, strong, well-developed, the hand that knows how to handle a tool, how to write, the hand that knows how to defend the body. The Bantu is also a strong hand. A powerful aid to the other hand. If one wants to pick up a heavy burden, both hands must help. With both hands together, engaged in the same effort, we can accomplish prodigies. To help our people, both hands must work together."

If the current policies of the Government of South Africa succeed in bringing "both hands" together to the job of decolonization instead of allowing them to become clenched fists in a fratricidal war; if these policies, humanized as they go, can save the Bantus from some part at least of the growing pains which handicap the new states and which are convincing even their friends that "Black Africa has made a bad start," then, despite the errors of apartheid, history will look with kindness on the policy of the Bantustans.

This is why the United Nations should spend its time on worthier projects than voting economic sanctions against South Africa, which are, incidentally, unenforceable. They should reexamine the Bantustan policy and possibly once again find an issue on which East and West can agree, as happened in 1947 when both blocs united for a short moment (a feat unique in United Nations history) to vote for the partition of Palestine and the creation of the Jewish state. The Negro state which is being born in the Transkei is every bit as legitimate as the state of Israel. This is why the elections, the flags raised in the Transkei, the Parliament in Umtata, are more than just pagentry to amuse the gallery. It is history in the making.

Translated from the French by Priscilla L. Buckley.

FOCUS

ON THE UNITED NATIONS

AND AFRICA

10   What the United Nations Could Do in Africa: An Affirmative View

PIETER LESSING

PIETER LESSING *is a South African-born British author, journalist, and broadcaster. As a foreign correspondent, he has lived and worked extensively in Communist countries. In recent years, in association with the British Broadcasting Corporation, he has made an intensive study of Africa and the African revolution. On two separate year-long fact-finding tours through the African continent, he covered 50,-000 miles by road and lived with African tribes.*

His books on Africa are The African Kaleidoscope, Africa's Red Harvest, *and* Only Hyenas Laugh *(which deals with the various experiments of black and white to live together in Africa). He has written extensively on Africa for the* Christian Science Monitor.

It is perhaps a generalization and an oversimplification to say that Africa is a continent with a chip on its shoulder. There is nevertheless much truth in it. It applies to Africa as a whole, to almost every separate country in Africa, and to most of the politically conscious people who live in it.

It applies as much to the Arabs in the north as to the whites in the south and the Africans in the center. It is only the size of the chip that varies from place to place.

In the newly emergent Africa the size varies with the degree of success or failure which independence has brought. The Congo started off in 1960, already severely handicapped by a good-sized chip and the subsequent failure of independence has increased it to incubus proportions. In the same year Nigeria started out on what might have been the same road, but month by month, as it becomes clear that the Nigerian experiment is, on balance, a success, the size of the chip is decreasing, and the people and their leaders therefore find it increasingly possible to think straight.

The inability to think straight is the biggest single problem in the New Africa. Bigotry, prejudice, intolerance, fanaticism and sometimes plain perversity confuse far too many vital issues at a time when clear thinking is perhaps Africa's greatest need. What is particularly unfortunate is that these impediments are by their very nature contagious, and the contagion has penetrated far-flung corners of the earth, corners from where, through the United Nations, the future of Africa is to some extent, and often very much, influenced.

Africa has always been a continent of paradoxes, but the last eight years have seen what is perhaps the greatest paradox in its whole history. For as far back as its history is known, Africa has been a continent of violence. Bloodshed, tyranny, cruelty—these have been the basic ingredients through the ages. And during the past decade Africa has seen the biggest revolution in history, a revolution which in scope eclipses that of France nearly two hundred years ago and that of Russia earlier this century. Yet this revolution, in this violent continent, has been carried through in the most peaceful manner possible, except in Algeria, which is not African but Mediterranean. In Africa proper there have, of course, been some killings, but with 200 million people on the march, sweeping away the old order, the few instances of bloodshed assume the proportions of no more than unfortunate incidents. The Congo has been the biggest single incident and for a while threatened to upset the picture, but the worst has by now probably happened there.

It is still too soon to say what the aftermath of the revolution will bring, but the fact should be recorded that the revolution did not begin with widespread bloodshed and was carried through, until this stage at least, with a remarkable lack of human sacrifice. Nevertheless, the consequences of independence have disappointed many, except perhaps those lucky enough to be in power, which means in effect those lucky enough to have won the last election before independence.

Yet, if one supports the dictum that Africa is for the Africans, then the deterioration of many standards must be accepted. That dictum must carry with it *ipso facto* the stipulation that the Africans must be left in peace to sort out their own affairs. Given time—an unspecified amount of time—a new order could be established by the Africans, more suited to the needs of the Africans or what their leaders regard as their needs in their specific conditions. This order would almost certainly not resemble that worked out over centuries in Britain to suit British conditions or temperament, or in France to suit French conditions or temperament, or in the United States to meet American needs, and so on. But still, provided that the dictum is accepted, as it is at the United Nations and in Washington, there can be no quarrel about that by outsiders. For this, however, the new Africa would have to be left in peace.

African Nationalism

In working out the new order, time and necessity would have taught their own lessons to Africa, such as the responsibility of ownership, indeed the sense of responsibility which is basic in any orderly society, and with it the need to develop economies which are less fragile and vulnerable, the need to invest in education and in roads and other forms of communication, instead of relying excessively, almost exclusively, on outside help. In this connection it is necessary to stress that I am dealing with the *new* Africa and not with the Arabs of the north who, apart from geographic location, belong to the Arab world rather than to Africa and who have an entirely different background and history. As yet there is for the new Africa no real stimulus to develop these qualities. Outside interests are willing to assume these burdens on behalf of emergent Africa, leaving the African leaders free to embark on the quicksands of emotional nationalism.

The term "African nationalism" today has an almost mystical connotation throughout the world, but it is in fact little more than a catchphrase. Even Pan-Africanism is an importation from the American Negro which until recently was to the African a meaningless concept. Nationalism implies a concept of nationhood with a deep sense of duty and service towards that nation, which can be overdone to the extent of chauvinism.

There is no *African* nation yet. Nor is there yet a Congolese nation or a Nigerian nation or an Ethiopian nation, and so on. There is, instead, a conglomeration of races; Nilotic, Hamitic, Bantu, Nilo-Hamitic; with different origins, different languages, customs, traditions, beliefs and, in many cases, a mutual hostility between them. Some have not been in Africa as long as the Portuguese have been. (Recently in Angola I met a white Portuguese whose family has had unbroken residence in Africa since the year 1183, without ever returning to Portugal.)

The only thing they have in common is approximately the same color of skin, and it is on this that the much-vaunted African nationalism is based. It is, in short, based on an intolerant color complex. It can be argued that the color complex was introduced into Africa by South Africa's practices and policies, but this is not a valid argument. France did not practice color discrimination; Ethiopia has been an independent kingdom for 4,000 years and, except for four brief years under the Italians, has always dealt with the white man as an inferior. Yet the color complex in, for example, Guinea, and in Ethiopia is, of course, more marked than among the Africans of South Africa. African nationalism, therefore, is in its practical expression perhaps the most vicious racialistic phenomenon of the postwar era, completely overshadowing in this respect Asian nationalism. Racialism is, in fact, its one rallying call.

Whatever the reason for the African's bitter color prejudices (and the former colonial powers must accept some of the blame), its effect, like that of all hatreds, is like a canker. It bedevils the African's judgment, the coherence of his thinking, his very logic. His color prejudice is, moreover, not directed merely towards the white South Africans or the white Portuguese, but tends to make him mistrust every white man, whether he be American, British, German or (to a lesser extent) Russian. This is a phenomenon which may pass in time, but not overnight. However, in the struggle for Africa it has become good politics for all interested outsiders to accept African nationalism as an almost sacred miracle of modern times, to accept the word of African leaders that it is something wholesome, and to treat it as a coherent force.

Another African paradox is that the African revolution

and the arrival of independence, the much-heralded death
of colonialism and imperialism, have resulted in a scramble for Africa more intense although more subtle than
that which marked the beginning of the imperialism of a
century ago.

A Many-sided Struggle

It is one of the most glaring examples of self-deception
today to believe that Africa can be, and is being, kept out
of the struggle between East and West. Nature is not inclined to tolerate a vacuum, and for all the assertion of
African nationalism, the departure of the European powers has left and will continue to leave a vacuum as the
withdrawal continues. The vacuum will, one way or the
other, be filled with as little delay as possible.

This is particularly true in a world which is daily shrinking, as nations become more interdependent and more economically intermingled, and where the term independence
has long since lost any meaning it ever had in Europe or
the United States. To be truly independent today requires
existence in a vacuum, and as the modern world has combined with nature to eliminate vacuums, it means that
Africa, all of it if possible, but if not, then piecemeal, must
inevitably be drawn into the sphere of influence of one or
the other of the rival contenders. As the world's second
largest continent with, potentially, some of the world's
greatest mineral riches, neither of the two world blocs can
afford to abandon Africa to the other. No relaxation in the
Cold War is likely to alter this basic fact.

It is, however, not a straightforward struggle between
two rival blocs. It is a many-sided conflict. On the Communist side, there is the intense rivalry between Russia
and China, already reflected in their often conflicting endeavors in Africa long before the open breach between

them. On the West's side, the interests and endeavors of the United States, Britain, France, West Germany and Italy do not coincide and are very often directly contradictory.

For Africa the result is, for the moment, the best of both worlds, or in this case many worlds. It becomes a simple matter to play off the one against the other when seeking aid for example. In ordinary business dealings it opens the way to excessive bribery and corruption. The European and American businessman seeking a contract in the new Africa who refuses to bribe his way might just as well save himself the trouble of making the attempt, and the bribery is increasing, not decreasing. It has proved to be not merely a passing phase. Add to this that any normal aid, even in the form of an ordinary loan, is usually for a project which in turn calls for the placing of contracts. It is rapidly becoming normal for the African official who has to place the contracts (normally paid for by foreign money in any case) to regard it as within his rights to emerge from the transactions considerably richer than before. Few business organizations active in Africa cannot today tell hair-raising stories of blatant blackmail. The worst examples so far are from West Africa.

Lest we are in too great a hurry to criticize this very human African weakness, let us remember two things. First, to the normal African there is nothing immoral in accepting a bribe. He does not look upon it as a bribe. Any position of authority in an African community has always carried with it many perquisites—as a right. Payment for favors shown or service rendered comes, to the African, within this same category. In European or American administrations there have been numerous glaring cases of bribery and corruption, and no doubt many more that have never received publicity. The mere fact that constant vigilance is necessary almost everywhere to guard against bribery makes it clear that this weakness is not particular to the African. But in Europe and the United States there are many normal checks, inherent in a multi-party democracy with a free press. Democracy itself having all but disappeared from all but two or three African countries, and with a free press nonexistent in nearly all cases, the normal checks are not there. If it were as easy to be corrupt in Britain and America as it is nearly everywhere in emergent Africa, there can be little doubt that corruption would in no time be considerably more prevalent than it is today.

In this connection the Communist bloc countries have a better record in Africa than the West. In the case of China the reason is quite simple: China does not have funds to squander on aid programs which she regards as superfluous, and Chinese businessmen and engineers do not seek contracts in Africa. In the case of Russia (and the European satellite states), aid is given only for specific projects which can help Russa's cause, and the aid is usually implemented by technicians or economic experts appointed by Russia (or one of the satellites). Much nevertheless goes to waste, as, for example, in Guinea and Ghana.

In at least two cases the Russian reward for providing economic aid has been extreme. In Guinea, in exchange for underwriting President Sékou Touré's economy, all economic planning as well as the implementation of the plans have been entrusted to Communist bloc economic experts. In Ghana, partly out of annoyance with the West's criticism of some of his extreme measures and its loss of confidence in him, and partly because Communist planning is nearer to his own brand of socialism, President Nkrumah has followed Sékou Touré's example. One or two other countries are going the same way, notably Mali and Somalia (the latter having been lately befriended particularly by Peking).

This does not mean that Ghana and Guinea have become Communist countries. The word "Communist" insofar as it refers to Africa should not be used too lightly. (This is a most unwise error made by the South African Government.) There are not many African *Communists* (Moscow's own assessment places the number at 50,000). But there is widespread and rapidly increasing Communist influence. The reason is simple. In order to accept the Communist dogma it is necessary to have a reasonable understanding of economics, which few Africans have. However, the Communist system, or any dictatorial system which practices state control and state ownership, does make sense, because it is much nearer to the African tribal way of life with its communal tribal property, tribal planning and obedience to the tribal chief. The deliberate attempts to break down the tribal system and to destroy the authority of the tribal chiefs have left many Africans bewildered. The Western democratic system and the concept of private enterprise and private capitalism are often a bit much to swallow in one gulp. To these Africans, leaving aside the mere opportunistic leaders, the Soviet system makes sense.

State Capitalism

On the economic side, it must be remembered that in the African countries there are few private investors and little private capital that can be used to launch any major project. All economic progress depends on state planning and on state capital, either borrowed outside the country or raised by taxation (leaving aside, of course, private industrial investment from outside, which must in any case conform to the general economic pattern laid down by the state). Inevitably the economy of a newly independent African state therefore is oriented towards socialism or, what is very much the same thing in modern practice, state capitalism. All that is therefore needed is a slight push by Moscow to upset a delicate balance to make the system swing towards Communist economic thinking. As the transition towards Communist economic thinking is a small step which can be taken almost unnoticed, the Communist world is better placed in this struggle than the West, whose task it is to prevent that slight swing, particularly as Western pressure is too often identified with "imperialism" or "neo-colonialism" and therefore resented and resisted.

The planners in Moscow are well aware of this. Professor Ivan Potekhin, the main architect of Russia's strategy in Africa, says in his *Africa Looks to the Future:* "An immediate task must be for the Soviet Union to secure the controlling influence in economic planning. . . . The State sector of African economies can play an important part in the reorganization of the way of life of the African peoples." I. Plyshevsky, a Soviet Foreign Ministry adviser on Africa and *Pravda*'s editor for African and Asian affairs, has added:

> Political independence does not signify the end of the struggle against imperialism, but its continuation in new conditions. In some African countries, however, state leadership has passed into the hands of vacillating, conciliatory elements, and even direct agents of the imperialists; here the struggle for real independence will, of course, be fought under more adverse conditions. But even in these circumstances, even if their political independence is to a certain extent merely formal, the countries in question have emerged from isolation into the mainstream of world development, wider opportunities have been opened for the growth of the national *bourgeoisie,* and the masses, enriched by the experience of the struggle against imperialism, are spurred on to greater activity.

Soviet progress in the quest defined by Potekhin is formidable in most of the new African states, but there is no need to list details here. Let it merely be added that Moscow has no objection to Western economic aid being provided to finance projects which had in the first place been suggested by Soviet economic advisers and accepted by African leaders, and then put forward as *African* projects. If the scheme is a success, thanks to Western aid, it serves to stress the soundness of Communist advice and the gain is in fact Russia's.

Who Makes Policy?

The inevitable question which arises is whether the United Nations (a) has a contribution to make in this connection, and (b) if so, what it can do.

There are two dangers. First, the new African states, if they stand together, already make up such a numerically strong bloc that there is a possibility that they may in effect dictate policy to the General Assembly and thereby run the United Nations for their own benefit. Second, if the United Nations Secretariat is strengthened to the extent that it can resist dictation by the General Assembly, then there is a danger of it becoming a colonial or imperialistic force itself, and, moreover, a power without responsibility. This danger was already inherent in the Congo operation. In this case the situation was saved largely by the fact that the Afro-Asian bloc which, with the support of the Communist bloc, could have dictated, was deeply divided internally and therefore unable to speak with one voice. Even so, there were some aspects of the Congo operation (part of which I witnessed personally) which produce an odd and uncomfortable reaction. The Congo operation proved that the controlling influence which the Security Council theoretically provides is not enough to exert any direct check on a Secretariat which takes the bit between its teeth; that it in fact can only lay down broad policy, capable of various interpretations. That cannot be remedied.

Yet if the United Nations is to play a significant role in Africa, it cannot be allowed to operate in a haphazard fashion. Its policies must be clearly defined, as well as its objectives. But who is to lay down policy? If the world organization is to be dominated numerically by the African bloc, will it not be the Africans themselves who lay down its African policy, exclusively for what it regards as its own benefit? It has not quite come to that yet, but the attempt is being made and the danger that it could succeed sooner or later is real. This is a disturbing thought if one considers that a sense of responsibility is often still absent from the African approach to matters of the moment, and that racialism, based on color, is still a prevailing sentiment.

Recently, while Portugal was being vigorously attacked during a debate, I asked a number of African leaders, all outspokenly critical of Portugal, if they could explain to me what Portugal's new policy in Africa is. Not one was even aware that there had been a sweeping change in Portugal's African policy eighteen months ago, and they were not interested in it either. Similarly, not one could explain South Africa's Bantustan policy; many had never heard of it. Yet these were the men trying to force the United Nations to take concerted action against South Africa and Portugal. If they had known the facts it would perhaps have made no difference to their attitude, but the axiom that you should know what you are talking about should apply to them no less than it is expected to apply to, say, the United States or British delegates to the United Nations.

Another glaring recent example was the Security Council session to deal with the fate of the Rhodesian Air Force. Action to prevent its being transferred to Southern Rhodesia was demanded by Ghana, whose information about the size and operational capacity of this small air force was so utterly wrong that, had other rules applied, Ghana could have been accused of contempt of the Security Council.

It is difficult for a sound, constructive policy to be shaped if the United Nations is to be used as a platform for irresponsible ranting and the expression of undisguised racialism, if the United Nations is to be the victim of blatant deception and self-deception, when too often the oratory and allegations appear to be designed to mislead rather than to inform. And particularly when the major world powers have to be careful not to offend the hypersensitivity of the African bloc, conscious of the Cold War that is being waged in Africa.

Equally dangerous is the idea that the West—or the United States, Britain, and others, separately—should attempt to use the United Nations as an instrument of policy in the East–West struggle taking place in Africa. Or that Russia should attempt to use the United Nations for that purpose. Such attempts have been made in the past, and sometimes they have succeeded, but it is a dangerous weapon and for the good of the United Nations as well as for the good of Africa, it should never be used.

It would similarly be unwise for the new African members to try to turn the United Nations into an instrument with which to keep out of Africa either Western or Communist influence. Some African leaders would try, understandably, to keep both out, some to keep out only the West, and some to keep out only the Communist bloc. That could, and almost certainly would, result in chaos.

All this does not mean that the United Nations should leave Africa alone. Africa has immense problems which must be solved before genuine progress becomes possible. At present these problems are not being solved because they can only be solved with outside help, but the outside help which Africa does receive in this connection is often nullified by the East–West struggle which serves as a background.

One aim, which would be of immense value to Africa in particular and the whole world in general, would be to bring Africa to the stage where she would be less at the mercy of the many conflicting forces at work. To get anywhere near this target, two requirements are basic and urgent. They are food and education. Africa is not only short of food, but what food is available seldom provides a balanced diet. The bad nutrition has far-reaching effects— on health, stamina, on the capacity to do sustained work at any task, and indirectly on political, even mental, equilibrium. Yet Africa is, potentially, not short of rich agricultural land. Ethiopia is one of the most fertile regions in the world, Tanganyika could treble its agricultural yield, Bechuanaland and even the seemingly barren Barotseland, parts of the Congo and Southern Sudan, the Cameroon Highlands and long reaches north of the Bangui River are all potentially rich food-yielding areas. Irrigation schemes are of course necessary, but they are costly. Equally necessary are modern agricultural techniques (plus modern equipment), which means endless instruction.

United Nations and Education

Education is a parallel case, and not only academic education. Technical training, training in practical administrative work, in trades and crafts, and so on, are all urgently needed. That Africans make excellent, highly skilled workmen when properly trained has been conclusively shown by the Portuguese in Angola and Mozambique, by Union Minière in Katanga, and by the copper mines in Northern Rhodesia. At present all training schemes offered by the outside world are regarded by many Africans as politically suspect, as forms of indoctrination, as part of the struggle to capture African allegiance. In many cases the suspicion is well-founded.

Would it, therefore, not be sounder if all aid of this kind could be channeled through the United Nations, through one or more of its specialized agencies? If the African countries are given an adequate degree of control over the direction of such special agencies much of the suspicion would disappear overnight. A condition, which would have to be agreed, would be that all the nations giving this type of aid would do so only through the medium of the United Nations, that no independent Russian, Czech, Polish, British, French, German or American program would be launched. There may be many practical objections, such as that it would upset the special relationship between Britain and those African countries who are members of the Commonwealth, or between France and most of the countries in the former French West and Equatorial Africas. At the same time, however, it would enable South Africa, who has a tremendous amount to offer the rest of Africa, to play a part in the real emancipation of the African continent, which is still only in the very early stages. It would also inevitably make Russia's contribution constructive.

It would be difficult to get agreement for such a project, but a start has to be made somewhere, and the United Nations is the most appropriate place for it to be made. Once the start has been made, the scheme could gradually be extended to a wider field of aid, such as economic development, while continuing to keep the United Nations out of the temptation to meddle in Africa's delicate and complicated political structures. How essential it is that the two should be kept separate was shown by the United

Nations' "presence" in the Congo, where the United Nations' left hand was destroying what its right hand was doing.

Such a scheme would by no means end the East–West struggle for the political allegiance of Africa, but would remove it from the fields in which it is to the immediate detriment of Africa and the Africans and is actually hampering progress. At some stage or other, higher education for Africans through scholarships (at present direct to European, American and Communist bloc universities) could also be placed under United Nations' supervision.

Formal education is of exceptional importance for more than the accepted conventional reasons. While Russia is not at this stage waging an ideological war *in* Africa, not asking the African masses to choose between two rival systems, not wasting time by attempting to preach Communism to the masses, indoctrination is undertaken as a long-term project among the youth. Russia is thinking farther ahead than the West appears to be doing. Moscow's policy, as first set out by Professor Potekhin in his *Africa Looks to the Future* (published in 1960), lays down that the leaders of new African states must be enticed into the Communist orbit by cajolery, bribery (by means of the economic offensive), flattery, offers of friendship and arms, and the exploitation of African nationalism. If in the process any of the leaders actually become converted to Communism, it will be a happy additional gain, but it is by no means at this stage essential to the cause.

The long-term task is to prepare the future leaders, the men who will take over from those who are in control today. To this purpose educational institutions throughout the Communist bloc are working to a concerted, centrally directed plan. Selected African students in universities as far apart as Karl Marx University in Leipzig, the University of November 17th in Prague, Moscow University as well as the Patrice Lumumba Friendship University (established in 1960), the Georgian Polytechnic Institute at Tiflis, the Central Asian State University at Tashkent, Uzbekistan, and others are being trained as the future leaders of their respective countries. Some of them are there with the blessing of their respective governments; many others have been recruited direct, without the co-operation or even the knowledge of their governments.

At a lower level, educational institutions in Africa are being penetrated. The aim for this policy was outlined at a conference in Prague in June 1961, the purpose being given as "to establish democratic and national school systems in the new countries in Africa . . . so as to ensure their independence" and "so as to fight cultural aggression where reactionary ideology and pedagogy are being forced on underdeveloped countries under the guise of cultural aid, especially as practiced by the U.S.A." (Notable success has so far been achieved in Guinea, Mali, Ghana and Somalia, and to a lesser extent Ethiopia.) Kenya is next on the priority list.

The question is how best to counter this offensive among the youth. British, West European and American universities play an important part and the contribution they are making is steadily increasing. They are doing their best to train more African students, and to give them better education, than the Communist countries are doing. Whether they are succeeding is open to doubt, because a climate is developing in which a Western-educated student is suspect of having become an imperialist or neo-colonialist stooge, whereas one trained in Russia or Eastern Europe (or China) is free of this taint. (The Western-educated person today too often has to lean backwards in the wrong direction to prove that he is not a "stooge.")

For Africa, however, the overriding question must be whether this kind of struggle is good for Africa. It cannot be. Two rival streams of educated young people, often with diametrically opposed orientations, being fed into a nation's lifestream, when they are in many cases the only sources of administrators and leaders, must perplex any young country. How, for instance, can a Moscow-trained Undersecretary for Finance be a good understudy to a Columbia-educated Minister of Finance, or, of course, the other way round (leaving aside the possibility of an outright conflict between them)? An early casualty must be the efficiency of the Ministry concerned. At best it must produce some confusion in an already confused Africa. Will it not be better, therefore, eventually to eliminate the Communist educational offensive rather than merely to try to counter it? The only way this could be done is by getting agreement through the United Nations to channel all educational aid through an agency of the United Nations. And, what is equally important, to get all African countries to agree to accept this kind of aid only through the medium of the United Nations. How the United Nations could regulate the award of scholarships, though a complicated matter, is outside the scope of this essay.

The Western Squabble

In considering the Communist penetration of Africa, it is a sobering thought that, despite all that has been said and written about it over a period of many years, the penetration did not start until less than five years ago. Until then there had been merely a negligible, haphazard, hit-or-miss dabbling in Africa by Moscow and Peking, which had not brought any tangible results. Only in 1960 was a definite policy formulated in Moscow, and at about the same time in Peking. The tremendous strides which have been made date mainly from that time.

It is tempting to speculate whether such strides would

have been possible if there had not been such a deep disagreement about Africa between the Western nations. If a large part of the West (including Britain) had not competed so strenuously with the Communist bloc in its efforts to jump headlong onto the racialistic African nationalist bandwagon but had instead made an attempt to distinguish between what was good and what was bad in the colonialism which they were so ready to condemn, and had first sought to find a sound basis for operating in Africa, the story would perhaps have been a little less distressing. Belgium, for instance, might have been more inclined to prepare the Congo better for independence, and perhaps Italy might have done so in Somalia, and Britain in Kenya.

The process still continues. Owing to the deeply conflicting attitudes of the major Western powers, the United Nations' approach to Africa so far has been less constructive than it could have been. But it is not yet too late for a change to be made. A first essential, however, must be a determination on the part of the more responsible members of the United Nations not to be so easily browbeaten by the more exuberantly fanatical representatives of smaller African nations who seek to use the United Nations as a sounding board to bolster their own egos. A beginning could be made if more Western leaders would admit that Africa is a more complicated continent than they had realized and that there are no easy solutions to the many problems, and that many of the African delegates do not represent the fount of all wisdom concerning Africa. And that this also applies to Western delegates, many of whom have never seen Africa or who have merely been taken on a conducted tour of the showpieces.

11 The Congo, Test Case For the United Nations: A Negative View

MUGUR D. VALAHU

MUGUR D. VALAHU, *born in Bucharest in 1920, is a naturalized American citizen. He holds a Doctorate of Jurisprudence from the University of Bucharest, a Doctorate of Jurisprudence, with specialization in International Law, from the University of Paris, and has studied at Georgetown University in Washington, D.C. The managing editor of a Bucharest weekly,* Cortina, *until its suppression by the Communist government in 1946, he practiced law in Bucharest until he escaped from Rumania in 1948.*

After working in Paris as a scriptwriter and speaker for Radio Diffusion Française, the British Broadcasting Corporation, and Radio Free Europe, he served as Secretary General of the Free Journalists Union (Paris), and contributed to Figaro, France-Soir, *and other European newspapers.*

In 1954 he became a writer and researcher with the Inter-Continent Research Forum in Washington, D.C., and in 1961 he commenced a two-year stay in Katanga as a representative for the Free World Forum and Foreign News Service. His book, The Katanga Circus, *was written on the basis of this experience. Besides fluency in European languages, he has a speaking knowledge of Kiswahili.*

There is a dream nowadays that a new worldwide war can be avoided because of the tremendous destructive potential of nuclear weapons. World war, a product of modern times, has not been prevented twice before, and it is hard to believe that we will succeed now. So long as there is more than one powerful nation struggling for hegemony on our tormented planet, world war will remain possible. The best prediction we can make, however, is that nations of conscience will attempt to postpone this periodical conflagration. It is therefore possible that mankind may live for some time in the precarious coexistence we call "cold war." Under these circumstances, many believe that the United Nations is the only means available to preserve the shaky peace which has prevailed since the end of the last holocaust.

Out of justified fear of nuclear destruction, many Americans have persuaded themselves that the United Nations is an instrument of peace which must be supported in spite of failures and shortcomings. There is a tendency to regard it as a sacrosanct organization, and for many years it has been an American endeavor to save its face. American officials have promised us with a certain stubbornness that the institution will improve itself and better its prospects as a real instrument of peace. It is therefore of capital importance to try to ascertain the actual usefulness of the United Nations in preventing world war or even local wars and skirmishes.

The United Nations was used by America in Korea through fortuitous circumstances. But troops in Korea were United Nations forces in name only; the fighting, the expense, and the sacrifice were borne by Americans, South Koreans and several battalions sent by the Free World in symbolic participation. The Communist bloc opposed the action; "neutralists" were unconcerned. Whether we call the war in Korea successful or not, the resistance to tyranny under the United Nations flag led many Americans to believe that the organization would engage in other actions on behalf of the Free World. This is also a dream. The composition of the United Nations is now different; it will never enter into a new operation against the Communists or one against "non-aligned" nations. The membership and the weight of influences have changed, and the Free World no longer has the same voice in the organization.

Nevertheless, America remains loyal to an institution which she can no longer control. For the past decade, the United Nations has acted on several occasions with no concern for peace as it is construed by the Free World. Instead of being an instrument of peace, the United Nations is more and more frequently accused of being a menace to peace and order. Substantial arguments are advanced by those who charge it with being simply a forum for the liberation of underdeveloped people without regard for realities. So-called colonialist powers have proved in various parts of the world the only ones capable of bringing freedom, progress and independence to underdeveloped areas, but in spite of this the United Nations concentrates its strength on disrupting these relationships. Moreover, say the same critics, the United Nations closes its eyes and turns a deaf ear to whatever happens in the Soviet zone of influence. Indeed, no measures are taken by the United Nations against the shameful existence of the Berlin Wall; no steps were taken against the bloody aggression perpetrated in Hungary by Soviet troops in 1956.

The list of United Nations refusals to act against *all* violators of peace is long and we shall discuss it later on. It is, however, unquestionable that in the last decade the United Nations has promoted only the Communist type of "peace" and that it has failed to be an instrument of peace in the hands of the Free World. If the Free World and its leader, the United States, are convinced that their democratic system and their Christian idealism are beneficial to the whole world, the United Nations we created and pay for must go along with us. No matter what Communist or unrealistic United Nations members may say, the Free World and America cannot afford to let the world institution slip over to the side of tyrants and irresponsible people—unless we want to bury ourselves, our security, and the peace and progress we have established.

An Analysis of the United Nations Intervention in the Congo

As one who has closely observed events in the Congo since its independence, I cannot suppress my astonishment at the facility with which the United Nations congratulates itself, calling its intervention in the former Belgian colony "an accomplished mission." Let us see the circumstances in which the United Nations intervened in the Congolese crisis.

In early July, 1960, only several days after the Belgian government emancipated the Congolese, the *Force Publique* mutinied against its Belgian officers and assaulted both the European and African population. The revolt took on serious proportions. Without discrimination hundreds were killed, tortured, robbed. Women, nuns were raped. Anarchy reached such a pitch that in a matter of days the former Belgian territory was emptied of most Europeans, who hurriedly escaped to neighboring countries. Frightened by the danger in which its subjects were living, Belgium activated paratroops based in the Congo to quell the chaos and prevent further murders and destruction of public and private property. The justified action of Belgium generated violent protests from Patrice Lumumba, the Congolese Prime Minister at that time, from Moscow, and from the Afro-Asian bloc, which in chorus accused Brussels of attempting recolonization. When independence was granted, Lumumba himself had permitted Belgium temporarily to maintain paratroopers in the Congo. These soldiers were to be withdrawn when their presence was rendered superfluous by an orderly and calm situation. A wise decision indeed, since the Congolese leaders themselves feared that independence would degenerate into tribal fightings and vindications and sundry other disturbances. But neither Lumumba nor the United Nations remembered this agreement when chaos erupted.

The United Nations was entreated by Lumumba to intervene against the Belgians because the Congolese leader was already turning pro-Communist and anti-white. On July, 17, 1960, the United Nations Security Council decided to send a force of 4,000 men to the Congo in order to prevent the so-called recolonization by Belgium. Troops from Ghana, Ethiopia and former French Guinea were rushed to Léopoldville. America backed the United Nations resolution, which at the outset had the purpose of replacing Belgian paratroopers in maintaining order. After several attempts to explain its justified position, Belgium withdrew its soldiers and by the end of July all military bases in the Congo were cleared. The United Nations action therefore was, from the beginning, directed against Belgium, which had brought civilization to the Congo, built up the country, made it notably prosperous, and in addition had granted generous, although untimely, independence to 14 million Congolese. America, allergic to a veto, did not exercise its right against this irresponsible resolution, although in a reverse situation Moscow would have done so, as it has done more than a hundred times when it thought its interests were threatened.

In Katanga, Tshombe, facing the chaos induced by

Lumumba, declared the secession of his province and clearly stated that there was no need for United Nations troops. Indeed, order in Katanga had been quickly restored by Belgian troops at Tshombe's request after a brief mutiny in Elizabethville by the local *Force Publique*. Katangans were in fact suspicious of United Nations troops of Ghanaian, Moroccan or Guinean origin. These troops appeared unreliable to them, belonging to pro-Communist, underdeveloped and anti-European countries. As a matter of fact, the United Nations was already helping Lumumba spread Communist agitation and incite Africans against Belgians, the backbone of any progress in that former colony. Tshombe, on the contrary, trusted his white advisors and even recruited European mercenaries. Meanwhile in North Katanga, Lumumba had stirred up the Baluba tribe against Tshombe, who had been legally elected Provincial President. Tshombe faced at that moment not only the chaotic situation of the rest of the Congo but also the threat of half a million Balubas, who were bands of killers. He therefore tried to train an army quickly and called upon European officers. At the peak of its strength the Katangan army had no more than three hundred mercenaries, including some Belgian career officers and a score or two of volunteers recruited among "colons" who had lived in the Congo for years.

Pushed by an irresponsible Congolese leader and his Soviet–Afro-Asian supporters, the United Nations obtusely commenced its mission. I watched this work from the beginning until its "successful accomplishment." For more than two years I observed the problems, the intentions and the actions of the United Nations, and I constantly tried to sift right from wrong. Today, after the "mission is accomplished," as Mr. Thant recently said, I still cannot find justification for the United Nations action nor hope for the future of the Congo following this intervention. People on both sides have been killed, damage has been done to property and to the morale of the population in Katanga at least, and huge sums of money have been spent. The Congo after four years of United Nations intervention was practically in the same deadlock as in July, 1960.

But let us go back to 1960, when United Nations troops arrived in Léopoldville as "saviors." Except for Katanga, Congo life was laden with anxiety and danger; Europeans had fled in mass; economic life had come to a standstill; tribal fighting, abuses by military and civilian officials were reported daily; inflation was soaring. In Léopoldville itself, however, a tense quietude replaced the previous disorder. In complicity with Communist-bloc representatives Lumumba was feverishly busy smashing the traditional structure of the country. Tribal chiefs were killed and authority was given to young African "Teddy boys," eager for politics. Rather than limit itself to its objectives of maintaining order, the United Nations ignored the tribal fights and the protection of the population outside the Léopoldville area, while abetting the Lumumba movement. It must be noted that through an agreement, the United States and the USSR abstained from sending either American or Communist forces to the Congo. The decision resulted in the use primarily of "neutral" and "noncommitted" troops. For many Americans, fearful of facing another Korean war, this agreement was better than nothing. But the "neutralists" engaged in political maneuvering on Lumumba's side. The Prime Minister insisted on Soviet aid and asked Communist diplomatic missions in Léopoldville to give him a hand.

In August, 1960, Dag Hammarskjöld, the late United Nations Secretary General, stated that "Katanga's secession was an internal political problem of the Congo and that the United Nations as a peace organization could not take one side or the other." "The United Nations," said Hammarskjöld, "cannot afford to influence personalities, groups or doctrinal schools which might prevent solution of an internal problem. I am convinced that difficulties can be avoided if the United Nations acts firmly, clearly and tactfully within the limits of its goals." Today we can say that none of Hammarskjöld's promises was respected by his organization. The United Nations action was not clear, nor was it tactfully handled in Katanga, nor did it limit itself to its initial objectives. The late United Nations Secretary General probably wanted to allay many fears, and in particular Tshombe's apprehension, and thus enable United Nations troops to enter Katanga. On August 12, another high official, Mr. Ralph Bunche, reiterated that "the United Nations cannot be used for the benefit of the Central Government and thus force on Tshombe's Provincial Government a specific behavior." Following these "clear" statements, Hammarskjöld was permitted by Tshombe to land in Elizabethville and to observe that there was no need of United Nations troops because order was not endangered. The matter of mercenaries was also a subject of discussion between Tshombe and the United Nations Chief. Hammarskjöld took advantage of Tshombe's naïveté and landed in Elizabethville with a company of Swedish soldiers, explained as "Mr. H.'s personal escort." The arrival of the first United Nations troops in Katanga was therefore made possible by a mixture of astuteness and perfidy on the part of the United Nations representative, since he had also assured Tshombe that no troops other than Swedes and Irish would be sent to Katanga. In accepting troops (Swedish and Irish), Tshombe was influenced by Dag Hammarskjöld's guarantees and by his own European technicians who trusted white United Nations troops. Soon afterwards, however, Indians, Ethiopians and Moroccans poured into Katanga. It was too late for Tshombe to oppose this action as the airport was already under United Nations control.

These are the circumstances in which the United Nations came to Katanga. By the end of 1962, 13,000 United Nations soldiers, mainly Indians, Ethiopians, Malaysians and Tunisians were stationed in Katanga, out of a total of roughly 20,000 men. Thus, 7,000 United Nations troops remained in the huge Congo to deal with anarchy, whereas 13,000 were in peaceful Katanga to deal with . . . secession. The United Nations Forces were recruited as follows: from India (5,300), Ethiopia (5,000), Malaysia (3,000), Nigeria (2,500), Tunisia (1,700). The rest came from Ghana, Sweden, Ireland, Canada, Italy, etc. The composition of United Nations troops in the Congo in itself illustrates the main preoccupation of the peace organization in the crisis: to crush Katanga and impose a political solution by force.

When Lumumba was fortunately eliminated from politics in the fall of 1960 by Congolese President Kasavubu, his Army Commander in Chief Mobutu, and other leaders, the Soviet Union in order to cover up the work of its agents in the United Nations declared that it was now against the United Nations action and refused to pay its dues. At this writing, Moscow still refuses to subscribe to United Nations expenses for the Congo operation. The facts surrounding Lumumba's death on Katangese soil in late January, 1961, are now neither here nor there. Of course, Tshombe and his supporters automatically became responsible for the death of the pro-Communist leader. In fact, however, Lumumba was practically dead when he stepped out of the plane which brought him from Léopoldville. Kasavubu, Mobutu and other prominent Congolese leaders decided, together with the South Kasai leader, Kalonji, to get rid of Lumumba. On the plane, Kalonji's men had cruelly, almost mortally, beaten up Lumumba.

The Soviet Union, blandly ignoring the millions killed

by its henchmen behind the Iron Curtain, started a violent campaign against Tshombe and Katanga, aided and abetted by its contingents in Africa and Asia. "Congo unity" was the specious slogan used to crush Katanga. Pressured by a storm of Soviet propaganda, the United Nations Security Council issued a resolution on February 21, 1961, directing its troops to expel Katanga's mercenaries, a thin disguise for the use of force to impose a political solution. We must remember that Tshombe, meanwhile, had been fairly successful in his war against the threatening Balubas. Utilizing his gendarmes and mercenaries, Tshombe occupied all the important centers in North Katanga, smashing Communist activity. Previously Tshombe had rallied to his cause Kasongo Nicmbo, the Baluba chief from Kamina and his 200,000 tribesmen. Moscow was angered but still hoped that Gizenga, one of Lumumba's aides, would succeed in taking over the Congo. This hope vanished rather rapidly, because Kasavubu and Mobutu aligned themselves with the Free World, and Tshombe liquidated pro-Lumumbist agitation in North Katanga. From that moment on Moscow knew that other means would have to be used.

Once the resolution for expelling mercenaries and Belgian officers from Katanga was adopted by the Security Council, the United Nations started its nefarious, useless work in this province. All attention, all effort was directed against Katanga, although the rest of the Congo was crippled by tribalism, economic disintegration, and administrative disorganization. In spite of all guarantees, the United Nations enthusiastically involved itself in forcing upon Katanga compulsory integration. The United Nations ignored Congolese realities and especially the Conference of Tananarive in March, 1961, which was on the point of bringing about reconciliation among all Congolese provinces and leaders on the basis of a loose federal constitution. This conference was, by the way, engineered by Tshombe and by Kasavubu, both strongly in favor of a Congolese Federation. Instead of encouraging this beginning of cooperation, the United Nations subtly exploited the inconsistencies of Congolese leaders and began crying, together with other Afro-Asian opponents, that the Congo must be united, by using force, if necessary, to expel all political and military advisers, all mercenaries, all hardcore Katangans, "the backbone" of secessionist activity, as the United Nations put it. There were, as I have said, three hundred officers and mercenaries and a score of "settler" volunteers, as well as a hurriedly recruited gendarmerie of 23,000 Africans, of whom at least 95 percent could be called anything but soldiers, so poorly were they trained. This gendarmerie and its mercenary corps was a nightmare to the United Nations. Thirteen thousand disciplined, well-trained, well-armed United Nations troops were frightened by this scarecrow army, and more than two years were wasted by the United Nations in trying to get rid of them and to end Katanga's autonomy. The first military attempt was initiated in September, 1961. It ended with the occupation by the United Nations of several administrative buildings of no importance, with many casualties on both sides, with the incredible capture of two hundred Irish United Nations soldiers and with a complete United Nations failure. In December, 1961, the second assault, a sequel to the first, was motivated by feelings of revenge and marked by innumerable incidents as senseless as they were useless. In both military actions, the United Nations disclosed not only its political intentions but its combat limitations and moral insolvency as well.

Let us try to enumerate the United Nations inadequacies, blunders and illegal acts during these two military operations:

A. Military unpreparedness. Ignorance of realities and lack of cooperation between units. Lack of fighting motivation.

B. Shooting at ambulances and murder of Red Cross personnel. Acts unrelated to legitimate military objectives, such as: murder and injury of civilians, robbery, rape. Occupation of hospitals. Damage to non-military objectives such as schools, hospitals, factories, private homes, etc. Theft of cars.

C. Encouragement of tribal dissensions by the opening of a dramatic Baluba refugee camp. Neglect in turning in criminals and thieves to proper authorities.

In addition to these acts, the United Nations bears the responsibility for the following consequences in the social and the political life of the Congo:

A. Deterioration of Katanga's economy and of social cooperation.

B. Increased hatred between Katangans and the rest of the Congo.

C. Increased distrust of and hatred against whites, and in particular against Americans.

D. Increased nationalist sentiment among Katangans.

E. Disorganization of the administration through expulsion of technicians.

I should stress, in connection with the operation of December, 1961, that during a period of almost three weeks the United Nations mortars and planes bombed and machine-gunned the city of Elizabethville with a population of 180,000, including 13,000 Europeans. The city was defended by 50 to 75 mercenaries and 200 to 300 gendarmes. More than 5,000 United Nations troops did not have the courage to enter the town and conquer it in a matter of hours but preferred instead to bomb it. This cowardice cannot be called anything other than criminal.

The third United Nations action was undertaken a year later and culminated in the capitulation of Katanga on January 14, 1963. This time the United Nations acted quickly. Casualties were reduced as gendarmes and mercenaries did not resist. Nevertheless, in marching on Jadotville, the United Nations risked the destruction of mining installations. Katangans, threatening a scorched earth policy, had previously loaded with dynamite all important plants, bridges, dams, etc. Fortunately, as a result of Tshombe's decision, major destructions were avoided.

The serious United Nations failures, prior to the integration of Katanga, are not limited to those I have mentioned. On the debit side we should also inscribe the following:

A. Unwillingness to cope with the anarchy and social and economic chaos in the rest of the Congo.

B. Inability to prevent atrocities by ANC (Congolese National Army) soldiers against United Nations personnel and white and African civilians. While the United Nations engaged in a war in Katanga and neglected the maintenance of order in the Congo, thirteen Italian United Nations pilots were butchered in Kindu by the ANC in November, 1961. A month later the same units massacred twenty-three missionaries in Kongolo on New Year's Eve, 1962. No reprisals were taken against these undisciplined troops by the United Nations, intent on forcing reintegration on Katanga.

C. False information and impermissible propaganda disseminated by United Nations officials in Katanga.

D. Undiplomatic behavior by United Nations officials toward Katangan leaders and Europeans, especially Belgian citizens. Arbitrary expulsion of technicians and arrests.

E. Overt assistance to the ANC in its invasion of North Katanga without any control exerted against undisciplined Congolese troops.

F. Irresponsible military action taken in early January, 1963, against Jadotville which could have resulted in the destruction of important mining installations. The United Nations itself gave as a pretext for the unwise operation faulty communications between Elizabethville Headquarters and Léopoldville or New York. The United Nations also admitted to having improvised steps which called for troops to occupy Jadotville quickly.

United Nations Accomplishments After the Integration of Katanga *

Once the capitulation of Katanga was obtained the United Nations began on the one hand to boast of its accomplished mission and on the other hand to withdraw its troops rapidly from the scene of the crime. Paradoxically, following its intervention in the Congo, the United Nations became a sort of *mal necessaire*. Order in Katanga was shaken as a result of the intervention, and gendarmes and bandits of all sorts were free to take the law in their own hands. The Central Government was unprepared to take over Katanga and the United Nations was eager to depart from the country, leaving the population to the mercy of the ANC. Inflation and economic chaos brought misery and unemployment. The Monetary Council, established and controlled by the United Nations, made some laudable efforts to redeem a chaotic situation. One cannot say, however, that there was any noticeable improvement

* The discussion in this section was written before the dramatic reversal in the Congo when Tshombe was called upon to try to salvage the situation depicted here and to contend with widespread rebellion among the tribes. It throws considerable light on the present strife.—Editor.

in the finances of the Congo agriculture and administration. The security of the population had not yet been insured by the United Nations or by the ANC. There were roads where acts of banditry were frequent. In the cities, thieves and bandits daily committed all sorts of misdeeds. Despite efforts by the United Nations, the population was still terrorized by unintegrated gendarmes, undisciplined ANC soldiers, and sometimes even by abusive United Nations troops, Ethiopians in particular. Tribal fighting continued because the United Nations was not omnipresent and the ANC was biased or careless. Although the Congolese Army and the police were unprepared to relieve the United Nations in its tasks, the organization reduced its soldiers from 20,000 to 8,000; only 4,000 were expected to stay in the Congo until mid-1964. The United Nations did not direct a serious collection of arms; many remained in the possession of former Congolese soldiers or non-integrated gendarmes. Too many automatic guns, machineguns and rifles were in the hands of Africans at a time when tribal fighting is fought not with spears and knives but with modern weapons.

It is obvious that maintenance of order in the troubled Congo is the key problem and that the United Nations bears the responsibility for the present insecurity. It wasted three years harrying Tshombe, instead of addressing itself to such important problems as the training of police and army, restoration of administration, control of smuggling, checking of inflation.

The United Nations is an organization with civil servants who are very well paid but the majority of whom lack motivation for developing a country like the Congo. Only Belgians have a real attachment for their colony. Although their motivation is part material, they retain a good portion of idealism, in spite of criticism and discouragement. The United Nations once again proved to be unrealistic and emotional: Congolese leaders understood that the problem of army training and of shaky administration could be solved only by Belgians. With regard to the ANC training, General Mobutu appealed to six free nations to assist in the reorganization of this essential military and police force. Italy, Belgium, Norway, Canada, Israel and America were invited to reorganize the Army, but the United Nations opposed Belgium and Israel. It is obvious that Moscow and the Arab States dictated to the United Nations on this score. Mobutu finally offered a compromise and requested that Nigeria train the police force. The United Nations has not yet given its agreement to the use of Belgian and Israeli officers, but Mobutu bypassed the United Nations and Belgian officers started their training job.

The United Nations has already supplied 1,800 technicians in various fields, including teaching. These technicians belong to fifty nations. Most of them have no notion of African realities other than a vague knowledge of French or native languages. Moreover, they are hired on the basis of one-year or two-year contracts and are better paid than Belgian technicians, a circumstance which incites dissension and jealousy. Most, if not all, of these technicians came to the Congo to make money for two years and then leave. They do not, therefore, have the same sense of responsibility and conscientiousness as Belgian technicians who have been in the Congo for years and who plan to stay as long as they are needed. Belgium has 2,200 technicians in the Congo today, financially supported by her.

During my stay in the Congo I personally noticed that many of the United Nations technicians have Communist convictions, and I am sure that they will not refrain from agitation or from inciting Africans against the Free World. A Communist or a pro-Communist, incidentally, has a much better chance of being hired by the United Nations than an anti-Communist (especially if the latter is a refugee from behind the Iron Curtain), since Soviet- and neutralist-bloc personnel have been appointed to important United Nations staffs responsible for the selection of technicians.

The United Nations forced the integration of Katanga in order to "keep the Congo united." Since integration, under the eyes of United Nations technicians, the Congo has been carved into twenty-three provinces of tribal origins with twenty-three provincial governments, each one having a dozen ministers. Expenses are tremendous and control by the Central Government over these provinces is impossible. The Belgians originally created six provinces; Tshombe wanted six federal provinces. The United Nations permitted this fragmentation into twenty-three provinces after spending three years to integrate one single rebellious province: Katanga.

In Katanga itself, Tshombe was practically forced to give up the presidency. He remained, however, the only popular and obeyed leader in Katanga where there are currently twelve political parties, three provinces, and total political confusion. Elections were scheduled for 1964. Innumerable leaders, demagogues, ambitious Africans are struggling for power since it means money. The political parties are one day for cooperation with the Central Government and the next day for unity of Katanga and full autonomy. Jason Sendwe, the opponent of Tshombe and Adoula's collaborator, was arrested recently after he spoke for the integration of Katanga and its fragmentation into two more provinces; now he wants unification.

The situation is similar in the rest of the Congo and the United Nations did not raise a finger to halt the burlesque. While treating Tshombe as an addled egg, it showed every consideration to irresponsible leaders. Thus, with United Nations blessing, Angolan rebels, trained near Léopoldville, make incursions on Angolan territory and terrorize the border population. At the United Nations, a whole campaign is now under way against Portugal, which is requested to give independence to four million underdeveloped and tribalistic Angolans. Having seen what happened in the Congo because of premature independence, the United Nations nevertheless encourages another chaotic situation in Africa.

When the United Nations Presents Its Own Picture

Recently the United Nations issued a long report on the situation in the Congo as a result of its activities. It is of course "pro-domo" pleading, an attempt to justify misdeeds and an occasion to praise itself. Let us take a look at this report. It reminds us, for instance, that "the fighting in which the United Nations was involved in September and in December, 1961, had been in self-defense and not aimed at putting an end to Katangese secession." Such blatant hypocrisy is laughable and disheartening.

The report continues: "At the end of June, 1962, the United Nations Advisory Committee had several meetings and discussed a future course of action. It endorsed the so-called U Thant Plan, which had been previously enforced by an appeal to Member States suggesting economic pressure on Katangan authorities while stressing that negotiation and conciliation must be sought by every possible means."

It is interesting to note that the U Thant Plan included in its first part the elaboration of a Congolese Federal Constitution. For three years, Tshombe asked for such a constitution to replace the inappropriate Belgian *Loi Fondamentale*. Although elaborated, the United Nations project of a Federal Constitution was not sent to the Congolese Parliament for ratification. The report clearly admits that the U Thant Plan was not subject to negotiation by Tshombe. It was therefore presented to Tshombe as an ultimatum, and this explains the third military action, its rapidity and its disregard of the Katangan point of view.

Details are not important now in the confused relationship that existed between Katanga and the United Nations. The fact is that the U Thant Plan was presented as an ultimatum, and 13,000 United Nations soldiers finally gathered courage in their hands and quickly ended the resistance by Katangans. They could easily have done this in September or December, 1961, and avoided sacrifices, killings and damage; but the United Nations had an amateurish approach to serious problems and blindly obeyed Moscow and other irresponsible members of the United Nations. Belgian officers, who were expelled, are now courteously invited to come back and train the Congolese. This invitation should have been issued when the Belgians came to quell the mutiny. Mercenaries were expelled, pursued and arrested by the United Nations; had they instead been hired to train the ANC, wars could have been avoided, and money and time saved.

It is hard indeed to find anything creditable in the United Nations operation unless one looks in the United Nations own report. We cannot close the chapter on United Nations self-adulation without quoting an incredible statement in the report: "The United Nations has closely adhered to two fundamental principles laid down by the Security Council. The mandate was largely fulfilled. First, it has respected the principle of no interference in the internal affairs of the Congo except for opposing secession in general; secondly, it has also adhered to the principle of avoiding the use of force for political purposes." How can a sensible man reconcile what the United Nations says in its report with what happened in the Congo and what was reported by so many witnesses?

The United Nations as the Playground of Communist and Underdeveloped Countries

The above-mentioned report has a special chapter on the Soviet Union's approach to the United Nations operation in the Congo. It states that "the Soviet delegate to the United Nations claimed that the Western Powers tried to bring Katangan separatists into the Central Government in order to preserve the position of their monopolies. The Soviet delegate also said that the Katangese problem remained unsolved both politically and economically." The Kremlin delegate is right, but he forgot to include the whole Congo. Nothing indeed has been solved politically and economically in the Congo because Moscow, the Afro-Asians and the United Nations were anxious to crush Tshombe and Katanga instead of proposing constructive action by the United Nations in cooperation with Belgium, the only country entitled to and capable of solving the problems that followed a premature independence. Moscow of course does not want a solution in the Congo but rather its ruin, since the Communists are particularly at home in chaotic situations where they can establish their tyranny. The Soviet delegate declared that police functions could not be justified under the United Nations Charter, that the Central Government could take over effectively, and therefore the United Nations forces were no longer necessary. What a contradiction! If nothing had been solved politically and economically in Katanga, it meant that order did not exist, that the ANC and the Central Government were as yet incapable of running the country. Once again Moscow pushed for further chaos.

Moscow talks a lot and refuses to pay a cent for the United Nations operation. The reasons for this are not difficult to find. When Lumumba and Gizenga were still in power, the Soviet Union was ready to pay. When they vanished from politics, Moscow refused to give any more money. When Gizenga still had a chance and established a government in Stanleyville, the Soviet Union sent him money, planes and technicians. The Soviet Union's subsequent refusal is explained by a simple calculation. Why pay money to the United Nations when American and other dreamers support it while the Communists can influence it directly or through the intermediary of various naïve Afro-Asian supporters? If the Soviet Union has not stepped in yet, it is only because she fears a failure as in Ghana, and she has other major objectives and troubles. The main objective is South America while the primary trouble is with China and the satellite governments. The groundwork for Communist penetration has meanwhile been prepared in the Congo: dissatisfaction with incapable African politicians increases; inflation soars while hundreds of thousands of unemployed and poor Congolese are crowding urban centers. Strikes can be expected, riots should be feared. Who will quell them?

The Soviet Union refuses to associate itself financially with the United Nations operation in the Congo because she has observed that America has clumsily and eagerly presented herself as the principal supporter of the United Nations. Half of the United Nations budget has been financed by the United States and more money is promised. Thus the responsibility for United Nations failure in the Congo will be imputed solely to America.

Up to now the United Nations has not saved or served the interests of the Free World in the Congo nor even the interests of the Congolese themselves. The position in the Congo is very shaky. If labor and Communist agitation starts, unless the United Nations stays in the Congo and wants to intervene, there is nothing to do but to call upon Belgium to reestablish its influence in its former colony. There is hope that the ANC will be trained quickly and will be capable of facing disturbances and any attempts at *coups d'état*. This is very much a hope and nothing else. The Afro-Asians and the Communist bloc, which pressed the United Nations to intervene in 1960 and to expel Belgian paratroopers, of course did not care what might occur. The situation today is the responsibility of those United Nations members who have the majority in their hands and who play with the destiny of peoples. The United Nations is the playground of Communist dictators and of underdeveloped nations. It is also an arena for propaganda and demogoguery, because the Afro-Asians are doing most of the talking—blasting the Western powers, blasting America, blasting colonialism and capitalism without discrimination. This is why the United Nations refuses to stand by the Free World and preserve the peace, the freedom, the progress that only the Free World is capable of giving to the whole world.

The West has built Africa and we are accused of colonialism and exploitation. We have brought in civilization and we are accused of barbarity. The Congo has its independence. And today European nations and America are attempting to rebuild, with money and technicians, what was destroyed by impatient Africans, agitated by their impatient brothers and by irresponsible Communists. Belgium is now requested to spend 100 million dollars to aid the Congolese. What has Moscow offered to Africa and to the rest of the underdeveloped countries except tyranny and propaganda? Yet today the United Nations is the instrument of Moscow abetted by the neutralists, the "noncommitted" countries who do not hesitate to accept money from those who have committed themselves to anti-Communism. What has the United Nations done to prevent Nasser from sending 20,000 soldiers, planes and armored cars to Yemen? The pro-Western Emir El Badr complained to the United Nations but no one listened to him. Hungary has been mortified by Soviet troops; the United Nations stood still. Eighty million East Europeans live in despair; the United Nations is not concerned. Indians threw the Portuguese from Goa into the sea; the United Nations had no time to deal with the problem. The Papua population in New Guinea is being coerced by Sukarno; the United Nations has never heard of such a thing. The United Nations is in Laos, but fighting is going on as Americans and pro-Western Indo-Chinese are killed under its passive eyes. All over the world the United Nations has nothing to say against Communists, against neutralists, against underdeveloped but aggressive nations.

The United Nations is, however, concerned with Katanga's secession, with Angola, and with South-African apartheid. Underdeveloped nations of the United Nations hold a meeting on tourism and find time to ask for the expulsion of Portugal and South Africa from the United Nations and from international commissions. Portugal must be excluded, say representatives from these underdeveloped countries, who forget that the Portuguese built a modern Angola out of the jungle. Communist tyrants such as Kadar, Gomulka, Dej, Khrushchev and their servants, are entitled to thunder in the United Nations against the Free World, but no neutralist member, no underdeveloped nation dares to condemn and to ask for the destruction of the Berlin wall where innocent persons are killed every day by Moscow's watchdogs. This is the United Nations approach to peace, to justice and to freedom.

It seems important, after having seen the moral performance of the sacrosanct organization of Mr. Thant in the Congo and all over the world, to look into the money spent by it. Since July, 1960, the United Nations has spent almost 300 million dollars, half of which was supplied by America. In addition America spent on aid to the Congo another 150 million dollars, and the charity has not yet ended. Belgium has paid up to now, and is willing to pay in the future, for 2,200 technicians working in the Congo. The expense is substantial, and Belgium is further requested to spend another 100 million dollars in the Congo. Twelve Western nations, among them West Germany, Britain, Italy, have offered to help the Congo restoration in one way or another. If the bulk of the aid comes from the Free World, what is the need of using the United Nations, an organization which seems interested primarily in facilitating Soviet-bloc maneuvers and propaganda?

Let us say that the Congo has escaped Soviet domination up to now because the Kremlin leaders know that Africans ask only for money and give only headaches in return. The Soviet Union has left to the Free World for the time being the problem of coping with troubles and charity in Africa. One day they will come to these underdeveloped countries, newly independent, and the Africans will be naïve enough to listen to their propaganda, to their Communist demagoguery. This is how the Soviet Union guides international matters in the United Nations, playing on the underdeveloped members with propaganda and waiting for the right moment to seize one country or another and establish the worst kind of colonialism . . . Communism.

Conclusion

An analysis of the United Nations intervention in the Congo has been essential in order to measure the usefulness of the institution and to evaluate our participation. I believe that in the minds of those who initiated this world forum the purpose was to have not only a peace instrument on hand but also one which could insure our own security, our own interests, our own mode of peace. There should be no confusion about the goals of this organization created primarily by Americans and with so much effort. Of course the United Nations must be an instrument of peace in the hands of the Free World. In implementing its goals, it must be a forum for freedom and progress for all. But for a decade the United Nations has proved to be the defender of Communist actions instead of a fighter against them. Under the pretext of liquidating menaces to peace, it has become involved in activities against the Free World. The theme of the United Nations now seems to be the liquidation of "colonialism," of the Western type of course, while the Soviet type of colonialism and slavery is ignored.

If the United Nations Charter can be regarded as highly idealistic, the motivations of many members have detracted from it. The Soviet Union is not entitled to the four voices it now has; other Communist delegations should be accredited only after having accepted an investigation of their so-called democracy. Either because membership has not been restricted and checked, or because United Nations representatives and civil servants follow the directives of their own countries, the United Nations approach to international problems and to peace is different from that which we had expected. We wanted an international organization which would preserve peace and defend the principles inscribed in the Charter. What we have is a conglomerate of national and bloc influences.

If the United Nations simply reflects opposing interests, and if needed action is blocked by the Soviet Union and its satellites, it is indisputable that it cannot serve the peace we aim for but only enhance the confusion which already exists and increase the danger of a new world war.

CONCLUSION

12   The United States, The United Nations, and Africa

JAMES BURNHAM

JAMES BURNHAM, *internationally known author, was formerly a Professor of Philosophy at New York University. He is a senior editor of* National Review *and writes a column on foreign and military policy.*

The Managerial Revolution *is his most widely known work; among his other books are* The Machiavellians, The Struggle for the World, Containment or Liberation? *and the recently published* Suicide of the West.

Any plausible account will list a good many contributory causes of the great postwar decolonizing wave that flooded out the Asian and African empires of the European powers. The social cracks opened on every continent by the two global wars were, certainly, a critical precondition. The emergence in some of the dependencies of a literate and ambitious local leadership, educated for the most part in the imperial centers; the cumulative effect of several generations of Marxian agitation and activity; the loss by the Western nations of their older sense of a positive civilizing mission, and its replacement by abstract humanitarian sentiment; the wartime promotions of local liberation movements to serve the strategic interest of one or another of the chief belligerents; the revolutionary antiimperialist operations of the Communist enterprise: all these were among the important factors. As significant as any of these, however, and quite probably indispensable to the outcome, was the policy of the United States.

It may be—though it is much less than certain—that the Dutch could not have held their South Seas empire at war's end in any case, but they had no chance at all once Washington made clear its support of Sukarno; just as fifteen years later they lost their last hope of keeping west New Guinea when Washington opted for *merdeka*. It was Eisenhower and Dulles, "leaders of the camp of imperialism and aggression," not Nasser or Khrushchev, who drove the British and French back from the Suez isthmus; and it was the Suez affair that proved to be the political and psychological as well as geographic trigger to the whirlwind decolonization of sub-Saharan Africa. There are instances—a very few —when, out of consideration for the troubles of a friend or ally, Washington counseled a somewhat more deliberate speed, or somewhat less massive bloodletting, in completing the imperial amputation; but the main line of United States policy throughout this postwar period has been to support anti-imperialism and decolonization when these have been directed against political domination by a European power.

There is no doubt, moreover, that the anti-imperialist posture of the government has been in accord with prevailing public opinion. Anti-imperialism and its accompanying proposals for the universal self-determination of nations and peoples are among the axioms of popular thinking, and have long been felt to be part of the tradition incorporated in American history. The United States had its origin, the story goes, in revolt against a colonialist and imperial power; and therefore we Americans feel an almost automatic sympathy for any other people that seeks liberty and independence by struggle against alien rule. These feelings unquestionably exist and have had much influence on the course of American foreign policy, but it must be confessed that the mode of their application to recent events has involved a highly selective use of earlier American history. If we seek our parallels not in the relation between the North American settlers and the English but in the relation between the Indians and the settlers, or if we merely note how the American West was actually brought under the sovereignty of the government established by the Philadelphia Constitution, we will not find it so easy to separate heroes from villains in the Asian and especially the African dramas of this postwar epoch.

Nevertheless, this well-known and widespread "New World feeling" has undoubtedly been one sustaining source of the anti-imperialist policy that the United States Government has in fact followed. Though its springs are rather historical than theoretical, it has tended to merge into similar feelings and attitudes derived from the ideology of modern liberalism, which—unlike the progenitor liberalism of the early nineteenth century—is systematically anti-imperialist and universally committed to ideals of self-determination, independence, liberty, equality, etc. for all peoples and nations, irrespective of race, color or creed.

Both these roots of American anti-imperialist policy—the historical (or pseudo-historical) and the ideological—might be called "disinterested." They are independent, at least formally, of the nation's economic, strategic and other material interests. They emerge as moral imperatives, telling Americans what is "right," not what is expedient. Nevertheless, it would be naïve to suppose that the explanation ends with these two, and that material interest has had no part to play. All Communists and most Europeans are very skeptical indeed concerning the moral dimension of American anti-imperialism. They judge that the moral principles are only a rationalizing and perhaps hypocritical cover for commercial interest; that American "anti-imperialism" is in reality "neo-imperialism."

Shortly after the end of the First World War, Leon Trotsky formulated the thesis that the result of another general war would be to make American imperialism the heir of a bankrupt British imperialism. In the event it has been European imperialism in its entirety that went into bankruptcy; and the United States has, in point of fact, taken over at least some of the assets. True enough, the United States has not attempted to replace European by American colonial rule in any formal sense. But even in political terms, a number of the Asian and African territories that were dependencies of European powers have swung to one degree or another inside the American sphere of interest. In not a few of the new nations that had been restricted economic preserves for the colonial power—Libya, Algeria, Morocco, Egypt, Ghana, the Congo and Nigeria are among African examples—the rapid growth of American trade, investment and economic influence has followed hard on the heels of political independence.

This does not mean, in spite of the interpretation given on doctrinaire or skeptical grounds by Communists and some West Europeans, that the United States is anywhere replacing Britain, France, the Netherlands or Belgium as colonial power. It was of the essence of the older colonialism that the government of the colonial region, however designated, should be in a formal sense a dependency of the government of the metropolitan state. The United States has not established and does not seek to establish such a formal political relationship. Under the older colonialism, moreover, the imperial power always enforced economic provisions that favored its own citizens and excluded or restricted economic participation in the colonial area by those outside the imperial structure. In decolonized Africa and Asia, American military support, political influence and governmental economic aid do undoubtedly serve in practice in many cases to ease the channel for American business and financial interests. But as in the case of the political relationship, the United States, resting on the traditional concept of "the Open Door," does not seek any formal structure of economic privilege.

If political and economic interests are, whether consciously recognized or not, among the ingredients of American anti-colonialism, there is one category of material interest, always prominent and often decisive in the older colonialism, that has been almost totally absent from American policy: what we may call "strategic interest." European colonial policy, in particular British and French policy, was always designed to secure the great strategic key points that control the main routes of trade and military deployment. European colonial history can be written more intelligibly in terms of strategic bases than of economic profits: Singapore, Casablanca, Suez, Trincomalee, Simontown, Khyber, Mers-el-Kebir, Gibraltar, Surabaya, Malta. . . . But the American exploitation of the breakup of the colonial system—especially in this most recent decade during which the African transformation has come— has been singularly, almost incredibly, free of coherent strategic concern. Of course it is true that with the development of air and aerospace power as the dominant military arm, a global multiplicity of bases becomes strategically less imperative—though not quite so secondary as some abstract strategists assume. But to say that fewer external bases are needed is not equivalent to the conclusion that none is necessary. We are still some years from the time when control of Suez, Dakar, Aden, Algiers, Cape Town and Zanzibar will be a matter of complete indifference. Nor can the secure use of a few air, and perhaps missile, bases in central Africa as well as in Africa's North and South, be yet judged strategically irrelevant.

The United States Government, in the past decade, has acted as if such strategic interests are of no significant concern. Not only has it made no effort to gain the use of bases for its own forces, it has made no serious attempt to continue the use of those to which it has had rights (as in Morocco and Turkey and, currently, in Libya). And it has actively intervened to bring an end to the use of key bases by allied powers: as in the cases of Suez, Algeria, Kamina (in the Congo), and by its present support of the campaign to end Western rule in Angola and South Africa. The United States endeavors to develop "an African policy"; but that policy is expected to operate, as it were, in a vacuum, without any leverage. The contrast with the current policy of the Communist bloc is striking. The bloc assumes that no African policy is conceivable without strategic levers—without acreage from which operations of whatever sort can be mounted. Therefore its continuous endeavor to establish and secure, chiefly by the methods of contemporary political and revolutionary warfare, the needed bases: in Egypt, Ghana, Algeria, Somalia, Zanzibar.

American policy toward the formerly colonial regions, toward Africa more specifically, has thus been a perplexing medley of the ideological and the practical: of traditional anti-colonial sentiment, abstract Liberal ideology, and indirectly pursued political and economic interest. It is hard to separate the elements distinctly from each other or to estimate their respective weights in the whole. In practice, the ideological aspirations sometimes conflict with and sometimes reinforce the material interests. Sometimes the ideological abstractions do seem little more than hypocrisy and sentimental illusion. In some measure, however, genuinely disinterested elements are present in the American policy. Americans, however deficient may be their understanding of the conditions of freedom and prosperity, do really wish that other nations and people should be free and prosperous. They are ready to give something from their own plenty to realize that wish, and within the policy of their government both the wish and the readiness have been reflected.

The main lines of American policy would presumably have been the same if the United Nations had not existed. The sentiment, ideology and interests expressed in the policy, in its contradictions and its absurdities as well as its positive features, all have sources independent of and prior to the United Nations. But the United Nations has in fact existed and does exist. It is a product in part of the very same ideology, interests and contradictions that enter into the American policy toward the formerly colonial regions. From its beginning, the United States has been chief nurse of the United Nations, and in late years the Presidents of the United States, both Republican and Democratic, have affirmed that "support of the UN is the first principle of U.S. foreign policy." United States anti-colonial policy, specifically, and its practical programs in relation to the decolonized regions have inevitably been linked with the United Nations and the United Nations' development.

What has been the effect of this linkage? Though the United Nations' voice was not required to induce the United States to support decolonization, the United Nations, as Mrs. Huxley remarks in this volume, has acted as "spur, goad and accelerator." Without the United Nations, the United States would unquestionably have favored independence for Algeria, Senegal, Nigeria, Kenya, the Congo and all or almost all the rest of Africa. But without the goading of the United Nations, the United States would almost certainly have advocated a slower pace in the achievement of independence: a pace that would have taken into account somewhat more rationally the position of the formerly colonial powers and their citizens, the needs of Western security and the condition of the local inhabitants. The United Nations' spur has helped urge the anti-colonial steed at a rate too fast not only for American and Western interest—that is obvious to everyone—but for the advance of the disinterested American ideals of genuine freedom and prosperity for all peoples. This could hardly have been stated more flatly than by the Secretary General of the United Nations himself in his June 30, 1964 report on the four-year United Nations Congo operation: "The United Nations has learned very much from its experience in the Congo thus far. . . . Fundamentally, what it has learned there is that the Congolese, in education, training and experience, and even in their understanding of the concept of nationhood, were unprepared to assume the responsibilities of nationhood." Accurate as is U Thant's summary of the content of the lesson, his own and his colleagues' conduct in the continuing instances of Angola, Mozambique, Southern Rhodesia and South Africa suggests that he is overly optimistic in believing that the United Nations has in truth "learned . . . from its experience."

The relation of the United Nations to the formerly colonial regions is complex and dialectical. The actions of the United Nations have accelerated the rush of the colonies to independence, and the ex-colonies have in turn swamped the United Nations, in particular the General Assembly which, largely because of United States initiative, has become the United Nations' primary organ. The General Assembly appears in its majority composition as a congress of the Third World, consisting for the most part of the transformed ex-colonies. The most convenient way of dealing with the Third World would seem to be by integral and loyal participation in the General Assembly and the United Nations' mechanism more generally. This is evidently the point of view prevailing in the State Department and guiding its conduct of United Nations affairs.

This point of view, unfortunately, is based on an illusion. The General Assembly is a myth compounded of myths. It is collectively a myth—derived from the triple fiction that there exists a "global will" or "interest of all mankind," an objective global law and an international force able to support that law. And the General Assembly is severally a myth because a good many of the constituent members are doubly fictions: the entities in the name of which many of the delegates speak are not truly "nations," and many of the delegates do not represent in any significant sense the conglomerate of persons within the geographical boundaries of these pseudo-nations. To call a couple of million persons, mostly illiterate, who have neither language nor customs nor laws nor history in common, who are not marked off by boundaries made meaningful by either geography or history, who do not have a viable economy or structure of public order or means of defense —to call them a "nation" is merely a play on words.

The curious truth is that a "liberated Africa" of several dozen "independent nations" exists *only* in the United Nations; it has no counterpart in reality. The phase of decolonization in sub-Saharan Africa is ending. There remains only the final act that will determine whether the wave carries all the way to the Cape or comes to rest at its present barrier. Meanwhile the phase of nation-building has hardly begun. No one can say how sub-Saharan Africa will be organized by the end of this century, into what framework of nations, empires, neo-colonies and tribal

jungles; but one may be quite certain that the frame will
be very different from today's.

Since the United Nations is a fiction that does not mirror
but distorts and falsifies the African reality, the United
States cannot deal effectively with Africa, or understand
what is going on in Africa, by concentrating attention on
the images in the mirror. This is the case no matter what
the content of United States policy may be: whatever the
objectives, they cannot be well served if a fiction is substituted for reality. Confusion results, above all, when a decision of the majority of the fanciful one-member, one-vote
General Assembly, representing nothing, is substituted for
a responsible decision by the legitimate government of the
most powerful nation on earth.

Damages consequent on a United Nations fixation, in
dealing with Africa, have already been frequently enough
demonstrated. The premature granting of independence,
which the United Nations has almost invariably fostered,
has harmed all interests, save those of savages and Communists for whom social breakdown is a blessing. The United
Nations' Secretary General, as we have noted, has written
the definitive commentary on what UN prodding meant
for the former Belgian Congo. If the United States Government had made its Congo decisions in relation to the
Congo itself rather than to "UN opinion," there is little
doubt that United States influence would have sought to
brake, not speed, the march toward independence; and
there is little likelihood that the United States would have
supported the folly of the military intervention. It is, or
surely should be, manifest that a sensible American policy
toward Angola, Mozambique, Southern Rhodesia and
South Africa—compatible with American and Western interests and with the interests of the local inhabitants—is not
being aided but made almost impossible by submission to

the demagogies of the Communist–Third World UN majority. Moreover, preoccupation with the generalized pseudo-Africa present in the United Nations diverts attention from the more fruitful positive task of developing closer, more active relations not with a fictional "Africa" but with this and that specific African country that is ready for mutually advantageous agreement.

It does not follow that the United States should altogether disregard the United Nations in formulating and carrying out its African policy. What is desirable is simply more common sense, and care to distinguish real objects from their shadows. If the United Nations is to serve the ends of United States policy—and if it cannot, then there is no justification for the United States to remain in the United Nations, except perhaps to sabotage it—then the United States Government ought to regard the United Nations as a potentially useful instrument, not as a sacrosanct principle. Even a fiction—and not all the United Nations organization is as fictional as the General Assembly—can be a useful instrument. There are educational, administrative and technological tasks in the development of decolonized Africa, objectively desirable from the standpoint of both the United States and the African peoples, that can, at least in some places, be carried out more acceptably under United Nations auspices than by a Western power operating in its own name. Let them be so handled—provided that the United Nations umbrella is not a mere cover for anti-Western intrigue, native corruption or bureaucratic waste and incompetence. But Americans will be well advised to keep one task well beyond UN reach, in their own hands exclusively: the task of deciding their own interest, course and destiny.